A **STAR** BOOK

The Spirit of Shropshire

BARRY FREEMAN WITH PHOTOGRAPHS BY **KATHLEEN FREEMAN**

First edition 2003

Published by:
Shropshire Newspapers Limited
Waterloo Road
Ketley
Telford TF1 5HU

ISBN 0 9546687 0 7

Printed by:
Precision Colour Printing, Halesfield, Telford

CONTENTS

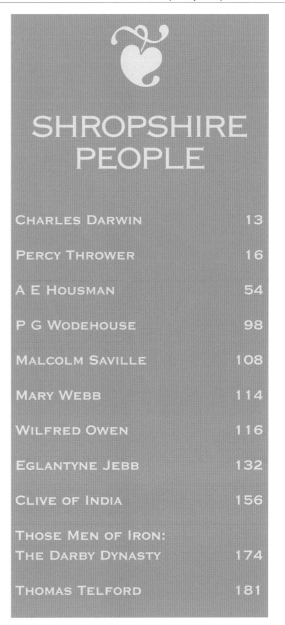

SHROPSHIRE PEOPLE

STARTING OUT

Shropshire is a big county. It is also a wonderfully rich and diverse county, full of fascinating places, beautiful scenery and friendly, helpful people.

There is something for everyone within its boundaries: up in the hills, the oldest places associated with human habitation; reminders of all subsequent periods of history – imposing seats of religious power, the hiding places of kings, the birthplace of the industrial revolution; and coming right up to date, there is dynamic Telford.

Here is a county which is proud of, and cherishes, its long history and the noble people who have made their mark down the centuries. But it is also a county determined not to stand still. It faces the 21st century with determination and confidence.

This book seeks to reveal all this and more, distilling the whole to the very essence of the county: the spirit of Shropshire.

Above left: Ironbridge.   *Above right: The Long Mynd.*
Left: Boscobel House.   *Right: Jackfield Bridge.*

HISTORIC SHREWSBURY

Few English shires are endowed with a county town as fascinating as Shrewsbury. Here is a treasure trove of vernacular architecture spanning the centuries: medieval, Tudor, Georgian and Victorian, all lining a fascinating maze of streets, alleys and squares.

Historic Shrewsbury is crammed within the confines of the great meander that is the River Severn, which provided a classic defensive site; a prudent choice for a location so close to the endlessly disputed Welsh border. As a consequence, medieval houses soar as high as timber-framed construction would allow, leaving a legacy of wonderfully ornate facades for us to enjoy and admire today.

Shrewsbury was the automatic choice for the start of our examination of the "spirit of Shropshire": centrally placed within the county and with a dozen roads radiating to all points of the compass, it is a delight to explore. The following pages contain a selection of the points of interest that visitors find particularly memorable.

Lord Hill (1772–1842) supported the Duke of Wellington at Waterloo, and his 133-foot column dominates the south-eastern approach to Shrewsbury. Said to be the world's tallest Doric column, it was completed in 1816 and is the focal point of the county council administrative area on the hill beyond Shrewsbury Abbey.

SHREWSBURY ABBEY CHURCH

LIKE so many former monastic churches, Shrewsbury Abbey remains grandly expensive, despite being shorn of its east end, transepts and extensive domestic buildings in the post-dissolution years. Further depredations were suffered a century later in the Civil War; the church was even used as a prison for Scots mercenaries after the final Royalist defeat at Worcester.

The last three centuries have generally been kinder to the Abbey Church, if not to its surroundings. Telford's realigned road of 1836 was laid over the site of the chapter house, cloisters and other buildings, but the nineteenth century saw several periods of restoration, culminating in the reinstatement of the east end in 1886–87. The Victorians' plans remain unfinished, however: the transepts included in the design have never been built.

Restoration of the tower in 1909 was the first structural undertaking of the twentieth century, but the demands of two world wars meant that nothing further could be done until the 1980s, when the Abbey Church was declared a scheduled monument.

Widespread public awareness of the former monastic way of life at Shrewsbury was created in 1977 with the publication of the first Brother Cadfael book by Ellis Peters (the *nom de plume* of Edith Pargeter), which was followed by a number of further titles and a popular television series.

SAINT WINEFRIDE

ANY major monastic foundation in the twelfth century aspired to possession of saintly relics, and "... the monks very much lamented among themselves that they were deficient in the relics of saints," according to Prior Robert of Shrewsbury in the 1130s.

Despite its many virtues, Shropshire had generated very few recognised saints and it was necessary to search westwards into Wales, a far more fruitful region. Here the monks found the remains of St Winefride, who had died in the seventh century. These relics were brought to Shrewsbury in 1137 and reinterred in a shrine.

Winefride means "blessed stream" in Welsh. The daughter of a Welsh prince, Winefride was unfortunate to arouse the anger of a young nobleman, Caradoc. In a rage, he drew his sword and severed her head, which rolled to a spot near a church where her uncle St Bueno was praying.

A well of pure water sprang from the spot where the head stopped. The extraordinarily resourceful St Bueno replaced his niece's head and she lived a further 15 years, becoming abbess of Gwytherin nunnery. The dastardly Caradoc fell down dead and the earth opened to swallow his body.

Today, St Winefride is remembered by the guild which supports the maintenance of the Abbey Church, and by the window designed and made by Jane Gray and installed in 1992.

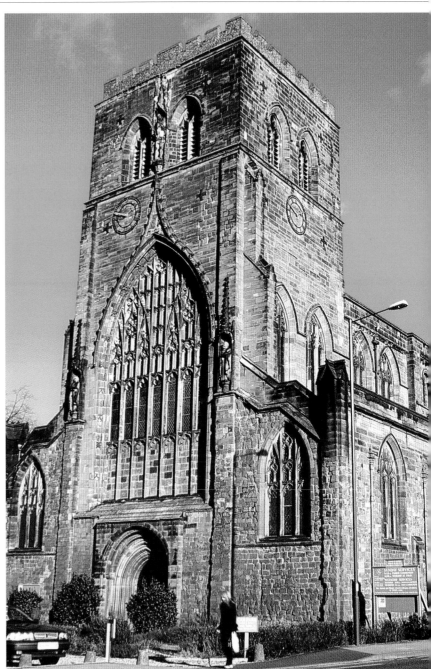

AN OASIS OF PEACE

ENTERING the Abbey Church, one is immediately enveloped by its cool, calm atmosphere, insulated from the bustle outside by the thick, soaring walls supported on massive Norman columns.

We should be grateful for the determination and dedication of our Norman forebears that they built such places and, in particular, for this all-important contribution to the spirit of Shropshire.

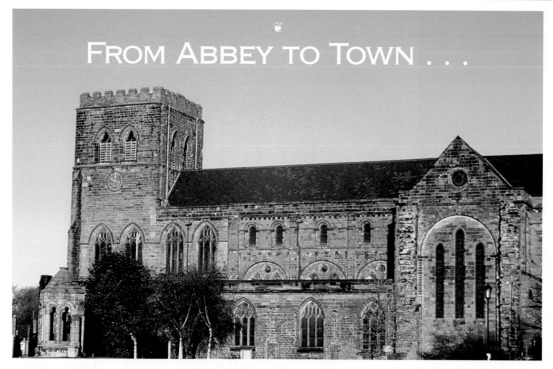

FROM ABBEY TO TOWN . . .

THE transept of the Abbey Church (south elevation, above) was infilled with the three-light window in the Pearson reconstruction of 1886–88, but the stumps of the original south transept remain. Pearson's plan for reconstructing the transept remain unrealised.

English Bridge (above right) provides the eastern access across the Severn and is an elegant Georgian stone structure, opened in 1774. Widened and modified in 1926, it replaced a medieval bridge which had houses built on it.

Abbey Gardens (right) provide the viewpoint across the river, with the spires of St Mary and St Alkmund rising into a cloudless, winter-morning sky.

ST ALKMUND'S Place (below) is one of the town centre's many hidden delights: a peaceful little garden area created from the former cemetery of St Alkmund's church. The lane to the right was once known as Burial Shut.

Bear Steps lead down to Fish Street and the timbered buildings were restored by the Civic Society in 1968.

Only the short medieval Fish Street separates the majestic towers of St Alkmund's and St Julian's (right). The latter was intended to have a spire but it was never added. Both churches were substantially rebuilt in the eighteenth century and St Julian's was enlarged in the 1840s. The towers, however, are much older. St Julian's in the foreground is of around 1200 in its two lower stages, with the top storey a century later. St Alkmund's retained its medieval tower when the Georgian rebuilding took place.

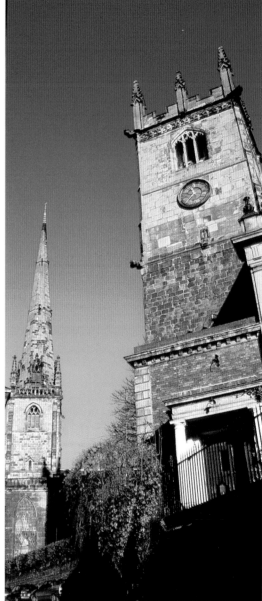

THE TOWN CENTRE

BUSY streets and quiet streets . . . that is one of Shrewsbury's most memorable and enjoyable features. The main commercial thoroughfares are always bustling, but turn a corner and the whole ambience changes instantly.

St John's Hill (left) is a rarity for any town: a street without parked cars. Consequently, the predominantly Georgian curved terraces can be enjoyed to the full.

Wyle Cop (lower left) is always busy: the reward is splendid timber framing of the fifteenth century, followed by the Georgian elegance of the Lion Hotel.

Pride Hill (below and opposite), thankfully pedestrianised, is

An Eclectic Mix

always thronged with people and displays a wonderful variety of facades above the modern shop fronts. At the lower end, High Street (right) has several excellent buildings facing the Square and Clive of India's statue. The picture shows Owen's Mansion of 1592, built for the wealthy wool merchant Richard Owen. To the side of it is the substantial stone facade of the Shropshire Fire Insurance offices of 1892.

These two buildings, side by side yet exactly three centuries apart in construction, provide an excellent example of how buildings of many periods sit happily together in historic Shrewsbury.

SHREWSBURY CASTLE

WINTER sunlight gives a delightfully warm glow to the main castle hall, refashioned by Telford in the 1790s for Sir William Pulteney. The grounds are pleasant, with a walkway leading up to Laura's Tower, also by Telford. From the side overlooking the street there is a panoramic view of the station facade.

Outside the gate is the imposing timber-framed building (below left), and through the archway is Council Court House (below), with an intriguing mix of gables and rooflines. In the background is the Presbyterian church.

CHARLES DARWIN

THE GEOLOGIST WHO SHOOK THE WORLD

IT is only Montford's statue of 1897 that really proclaims Shrewsbury as the town that nurtured young Charles Darwin (1809–1882) for his first 16 years. Yet here was a man who possibly exerted more influence on how we see ourselves and our planet, than any other person in the past thousand years.

It should not be difficult to appreciate the profound trauma experienced throughout society when Darwin published *On the Origin of Species by Natural Selection* in 1859. Overnight it turned on its head the virtually unchallenged assumption that the creation of the world was a six-day wonder. Opposition was widespread and vigorous from pulpits, the press and other would-be opinion formers. Reason steadily took hold, however, after *The Descent of Man* followed in 1871.

Charles Darwin benefited from an interesting lineage. His parents' marriage had united two wealthy pottery families: his father was a member of the Darwin family, owners of the Etruria pottery, and his mother was a Wedgwood. It had been expected that Charles would follow his father and elder brother into the medical profession but, after some medical studies at Edinburgh and a further three years at Cambridge studying for the church, he decided that neither career was what he wanted.

At Cambridge, however, Charles Darwin met the men who were to ignite his real passions: geology and botany. Professor Adam Sedgewick introduced him to field studies of rocks and fossils, and Professor Henslow secured for him the position of official naturalist on HMS Beagle for its epic five-year voyage to the southern hemisphere.

The huge collection of specimens and notebooks accumulated on this voyage were the foundation for Darwin's lifelong work as he steadily grew in stature to become one of the giants of Victorian England – the schoolboy from Shrewsbury who opened mankind's eyes to the world as it really is.

St Chad's

SAINT Chad's is an exciting and memorable church . . . for its striking architecture, its sumptuous interior and its unrivalled setting overlooking the Dingle and the great sweep of the River Severn.

The three pictures here show what are possibly the most abiding images of St Chad's: the main entrance flanked by four elegant Tuscan columns; the striking church interior looking towards the altar; and (opposite) the view from across the pool in the Dingle.

PERCY THROWER

THE NATION'S HEAD GARDENER

PERCY Thrower was born in 1913, the second son of Harry and Maud Thrower on the estate of Little Horwood in Buckinghamshire.

Like his father, he wanted to be a head gardener, and went through a rigorous apprenticeship on the royal estate of Windsor under Charles Cook – who was later to become his father-in-law.

From Windsor, he moved to Leeds and then to Derby, before coming to Shrewsbury in January 1946 as the youngest park superintendent of that time. He was given the responsibility of returning the world-famous Quarry Park and Dingle to their original glory after the neglect of the war years.

Shrewsbury was to be a stepping-stone to advance his horticultural career, and he planned to stay for only a few years. However, he fell in love with the region and with the friendly people, and made his home here for the next 42 years until his death in 1988.

In the 1950s he started his radio career, and later became a prominent gardening

personality on television, often being referred to as the "nation's head gardener".

Percy took great pride in his adopted town of Shrewsbury, producing the renowned floral displays in and around the county town. Perhaps the most colourful was the Dingle (pictured opposite); the oasis-hidden treasure situated in a dell in the heart of the Quarry. These colourful,

manicured ornamental gardens today remain much as they were in his time. Many of the early TV Gardening Club programmes were filmed from the Dingle, as well as from his private garden developed from a bare field site on the northern outskirts of Shrewsbury.

The world-famous Shrewsbury Flower Show is held each August in the Quarry, and he was horticultural adviser on the show committee for all the time he lived in the town, holding the office of chairman in 1975. He was immensely proud of the very high standard and plant quality always exhibited at the show. He was also for many years an exhibitor in the main Quarry Marquee under the banner of Percy Thrower's Gardening Centre, where he staged the very large fuchsia gardens which won him the prized Edith Aveling trophy for best in show on numerous occasions.

Percy Thrower's Gardening Centre to the south of the town opened in 1969. It still carries his name and has considerable family involvement.

MARGARET THROWER

SHREWSBURY FLOWER SHOW

IT has been called "the finest summer flower show in the British Isles." And so it is! More than three million blooms from the nation's top growers, both professional and amateur, more than justify this accolade from independent judges.

The country's leading show can also claim what must be the most delightful setting: Shrewsbury's beautiful 29-acre Quarry Park, with the magnificent sunken Dingle gardens providing a visually stunning centrepiece.

For more than a century, Shrewsbury has been hosting this two-day show in mid-August, nowadays receiving some 100,000 visitors each year as evidence of its perennial popularity.

More than a flower show, the non-stop arena programme includes military bands, top-grade showjumping, choirs and special entertainments for children as well as the beautifully presented marquees. Finally each evening, the whole of Shrewsbury is lit up by one of the most spectacular fireworks displays to be enjoyed anywhere.

CONSERVING SHROPSHIRE'S HERITAGE

The Long Mynd (above) is one of the jewels in Shropshire's crown.

Cardingmill Valley (right) has long been a popular attraction.

The following pages portray the landscapes and buildings of Shropshire which are in the care of four organisations: The National Trust, English Heritage, The Churches Conservation Trust and Shropshire Wildlife Trust.

The National Trust owns Cardingmill Valley and a large tract of the central area of the Long Mynd, one of England's most dramatic landscape features. It is a priceless element of Shropshire's heritage, both historically and ecologically.

Rich in archaeological sites from the Bronze and Iron Ages and from medieval times, it is also designated both as an area of outstanding natural beauty and as a site of special scientific interest.

❦
ATTINGHAM PARK

ATTINGHAM Park is a neo-classical mansion set in a beautiful landscaped deer park. The elegant house was built in 1785 for the first Lord Berwick to the design of George Steuart, and has a picture gallery by John Nash. The magnificent Regency interiors contain collection of ambassadorial silver, Italian furniture, and Grand Tour paintings.

After the death of Noel Hill in 1789, the hall was completed and furnished by his son, the second Lord Berwick, whose chief pleasure in life was buying and commissioning art. His extravagance, along with that of his wife, led to bankruptcy and in 1827 there was a sale of almost the entire contents of the hall.

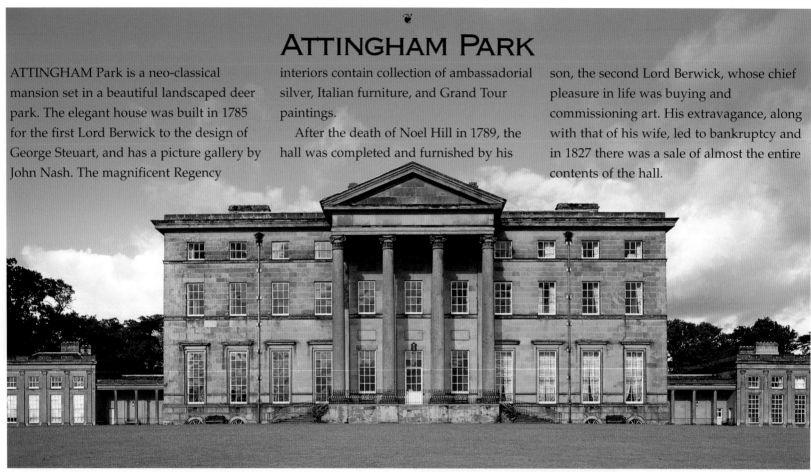

Home to eight Lords Berwick before augmenting the National Trust's portfolio of properties, Attingham Park sits in magnificent parkland. Opposite: the drawing room.

The house was then leased to the third Lord Berwick who had been a diplomat in Italy for 25 years, and it was he who brought the fine collections to Attingham that can be seen today. The house was given to the National Trust in 1947 after the death of the eighth Lord Berwick who, with his wife Teresa Hulton, had renewed and enhanced the interior of the house.

The magnificent park was landscaped by Humphry Repton in 1797. Repton's scheme produced a seemingly natural, pastoral landscape, and created the impression of limitless ownership. Visitors to Attingham Park can enjoy the miles of woodland and riverside walks around the beautifully landscaped park and along the River Tern.

SUNNYCROFT

SUNNYCROFT is a late-Victorian gentleman's suburban villa, typical of the many thousands of such houses that were built for prosperous businessmen and professionals on the fringes of Victorian towns and cities. It is one of the very few such properties to have survived largely unaltered complete with its contents, of which a remarkable range remain.

The substantial, detached brick mansion lies on the edge of the market town of Wellington, and encapsulates a way of life that was at the heart of British society between 1850 and 1939. It was bequeathed to the National Trust by Joan Lander in 1997.

The earliest part of Sunnycroft was built in 1880 for J G Wackrill, the founder of the Shropshire Brewery in Watling Street. In the early 1890s it was bought by Mary Jane Slaney, the widow of a successful wine-and-spirit merchant who owned Slaney's vaults in Wellington. When Mary Jane died, her brother-in-law J V T Lander bought it, and the Lander family lived at Sunnycroft for three generations. The memories and relics of their time there during the inter-war years, including the diaries kept by Joan

Lander, bring the property to life today.

As a provincial villa, Sunnycroft's design reflects the patterns and concerns of small-town life. It includes an imposing staircase hall, dining room and billiard room but no library, suggesting that social life was more important to the Slaneys and Landers than displays of art or culture.

The garden is divided into areas, carefully separated and arranged, with a clearly defined function. The long driveway is planted alternately with Wellingtonia redwoods and coppiced limes. Immediately surrounding the house are ornamental gardens which include the rose garden, the conservatory, the shrubbery and herbaceous borders. "Useful" parts of the garden are arranged out of sight of the main rooms of the house. The tomato house and vinery are situated behind the conservatory and the orchards and chicken pens lie to the south of the shrubbery. There are also stables, coachhouse, pigsties and fruit- and vegetable gardens.

BENTHALL HALL

BENTHALL Hall is a sixteenth-century stone house situated on a plateau above the River Severn. The property has mullioned and transomed windows and a stunning interior with a carved oak staircase, decorated plaster ceiling and oak panelling. There is a carefully restored plantsman's garden, old kitchen garden and a Restoration church.

The property was given to the National Trust in 1958 by Mrs J Floyer Benthall and endowed by Sir Edward Benthall. A further 8.4 hectares of woodland was given by the late Sir Paul Benthall.

DUDMASTON HALL

THE house, attributed to the architect Frances Smith of Warwick, was probably begun by Sir Thomas Wolryche in 1695 and largely built by the time of his early death in 1701.

In the 1820s the roofline was altered and pediments and a parapet were added. At the same time, remodelling was commissioned by Geoffrey Wolryche-Whitmore and the staircase and library were formed and the windows of the garden front enlarged and reglazed. The house remained in the family until Rachel Labouchere, the niece of a Wolryche-Whitmore, gave the house to the National Trust in 1978.

The intimate family rooms in the late-seventeenth-century mansion contain fine furniture and Dutch flower paintings, as well as a collection of historical costumes. Visitors can also discover the Labouchere collection – one of Britain's most important public collections of contemporary paintings and sculpture in a country-house setting.

Photographs, drawings and writings by leading naturalist Frances Pitt (1888–1964) are displayed in the Housekeeper's Room.

Frances was born near Bridgnorth and wrote many books and articles; she was a contributor to *Country Life* for more than 50 years. (Further items relating to Frances Pitt are to be found at Ludlow Museum.)

The delightful gardens are a mass of colour in spring, and there are extensive walks across the historic estate.

Above: The library at Dudmaston.

Opposite: Dudmaston has its roots in the latter part of the seventeenth century but has been extensively reworked over the years.

THE LONG MYND

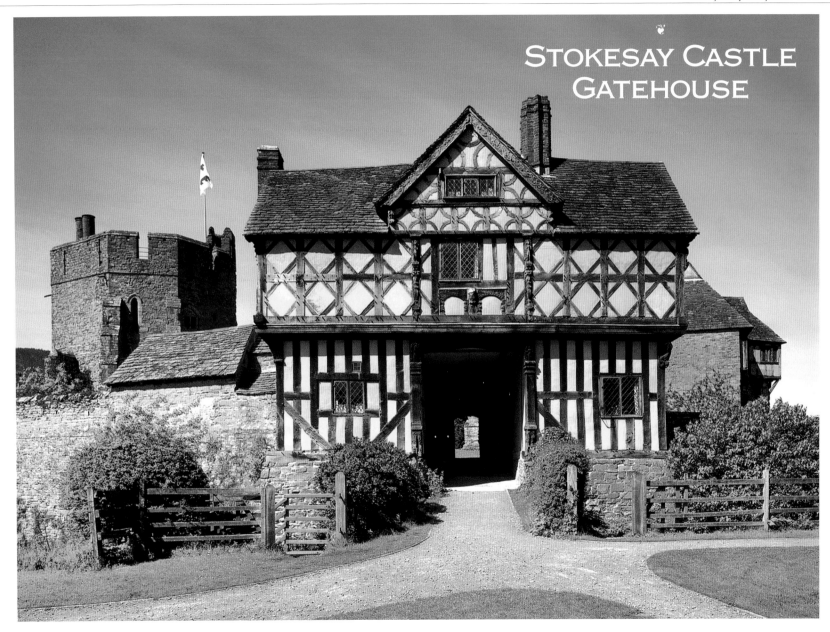

STOKESAY

STOKESAY is one of the earliest surviving fortified manor houses in the country – and one of the best known. Most of the buildings and walls we see today would, however, have had little military value, being too insubstantial to resist serious onslaught.

This was in fact the case in the Civil War, when the castle was surrendered to a Parliamentary force in 1645 because the walls would not stand up to cannon fire. The walls were then demolished, subsequently being replaced by even thinner walls.

The attractive gatehouse pictured on the previous page is probably late-sixteenth century, highly ornate but again lacking military value; the earlier gatehouse would probably have been a much more substantial stone structure.

Together with the adjacent church of St John Baptist, extensively rebuilt following Civil War damage, Stokesay provides one of the most popular and evocative sites in Shropshire.

WROXETER: ROMAN REMAINS

LIKE Stokesay, Wroxeter Roman City is a site of national importance, and extremely evocative. At its height, it was the fourth largest settlement in Roman Britain.

Called Viroconium (also Uriconium), the city was founded around AD60 as a provincial capital, and its period of most vigorous development was from 120 onwards following a visit to Britain of Emperor Hadrian. At that time public buildings, large townhouses and strong defences were constructed.

For more than a century, up to about 250, Viroconium was a prosperous city. Then, however, as in the rest of Roman Britain, demoralisation and decay set in. Firm direction from Rome became increasingly scarce and barbarian invasions steadily eroded Roman control.

Viroconium was abandoned in the early fifth century and subsequently became a source of ready-worked building stone for the developing Anglo-Saxon town of Shrewsbury.

> Today the Roman and his trouble
> Are ashes under Uricon.
>
> *A Shropshire Lad XXXI*

A view of the baths area showing the tepidarium, caldarium and frigidarium, and some of the underfloor pillars of the hypocaust.

RELICS OF THE DISSOLUTION

HERE are some more highly evocative sites, recalling the spirit of Shropshire in pre-Dissolution centuries. The county has a rich endowment of monastic remains. These sites, coupled with some knowledge and a lot of imagination, provide a vivid picture of the extent of their building complexes and the influence they exerted on everyone's life, from the most powerful families in the land down.

Seen from our latter-day heritage-conscious perspective, the dissolution of the monasteries can be viewed primarily as an episode of unparalleled vandalism. For Henry VIII, however, it was an economic and political imperative. Having broken with Rome, he simply could not afford to leave the monastic system intact.

Walk around to appreciate the sheer scale of these buildings and the extent of these sites, and you will realise what a force in the land they were. And this was not just a British network: it stretched in an unbroken chain throughout western Europe directly to Rome. Written and verbal communication was highly developed throughout the monastic network. The common language was Latin, which was not generally understood by the rest of the population. So long as this network remained intact, Henry could never rest easily; it had to be destroyed.

The Dissolution was not an isolated event. Throughout history people have destroyed the buildings of their adversaries. It happened in the following century when many castles were deliberately damaged to stop them being repaired. Our ruined monasteries are a monument to a phase in history.

Above: Buildwas Abbey from the south-west, showing the extent of the nave with its mid-twelfth-century sturdy columns. The abbey was founded in 1135 for monks from Savigny, who merged with the Cistercian order in 1147.

Facing page, left: Haughmond Abbey, showing the abbot's hall and private rooms. Founded around 1135, the property was sold to Sir Rowland Hill, Lord Mayor of London, after the Dissolution.

Facing page, right: Wenlock Priory looking east along the nave, showing the three walls of the south transept and the remaining west wall of the north transept. The original seventh-century nunnery was destroyed by the Danes in the 870s. The foundation was re-established shortly after the Conquest but the remains we have today are of late-Norman and early-English rebuilding.

BOSCOBEL HOUSE

THIS is a house which has become famous for one of those easily memorised nuggets of historical trivia: in this case, that King Charles hid in an oak tree. Doubtless many of us would be hard-pressed to explain when or why – or possibly even to hazard a guess at whether the king in question was Charles I or Charles II!

Boscobel was a Catholic house, built around 1600 and equipped with concealed hiding places. After the disaster at Worcester in 1651, Charles II was advised to seek refuge at Boscobel, which had already harboured other Royalist fugitives. The story runs that he hid in a nearby oak during the day and in one of the hiding places in the house at night.

The ruse apparently worked: the monarchy was eventually restored and the question of what to call innumerable hostelries throughout the country was resolved!

Above: A general view of the house across the small formal garden.

Right: The Squire's Room.

St Mary Magdalene, Battlefield, Shrewsbury. The magnificent hammer-beam roof, the reredos and all the fittings and furnishings were installed by the distinguished local architect S Pountney Smith as a result of an extensive restoration in the 1860s.

THE CHURCHES CONSERVATION TRUST

THE Churches Conservation Trust cares for and promotes public access to more than 320 churches in England; churches are chosen for their historic, archaeological or architectural importance.

A thousand years of English history can be discovered within their walls. Some are in the heart of cities; others in magnificent or remote countryside. Each has something special to offer the visitor: brilliant stained glass; fascinating monuments to the men and women of earlier times; exquisite craftsmanship; or simply the serenity of an ancient building in a peaceful setting where people have prayed for centuries.

They remain consecrated, although they are no longer needed for worship, and most have occasional services. Many host concerts, craft fairs, flower festivals and educational events.

Everyone is welcome to visit the churches. They are either open daily or there will be a keyholder nearby for those that are kept locked. All the trust's churches have guidebooks and free leaflets about other trust churches.

There are eight churches in the trust's care in Shropshire.

HANNAH MOSS

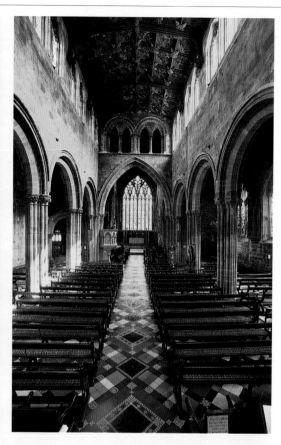

St Leonard's, Bridgnorth. The hammer-beam roof dates from 1662 but the majority of the building is mid-Victorian, completed in 1862. It is full of rich fittings, a glorious monument to the priests and scholars associated with this magnificent church.

St Mary the Virgin, Shrewsbury. This is the largest church in Shrewsbury, built mainly in the thirteenth century. It possesses an exceptionally rich collection of stained glass, mainly from continental Europe. The most memorable is the Jesse window in the chancel, made in the fourteenth century. The picture (centre) shows the panel of King Solomon; other panels depict figures of Old Testament kings and prophets in brilliantly vibrant colours.
In the nave (above right), the finest features are the slender columns of the early-thirteenth-century arcades and the fifteenth-century carved-oak ceiling. The ceiling bosses depict animals, birds and angels.
The superb Victorian tiles provide warmth and richness.

Inset: St Andrew's, Wroxeter. The church is built on the site of Roman Viroconium and incorporates Roman stones and, most prominently, the two pillars re-used as gateposts that can be seen in the picture. Features of successive phases of renovation and alteration range from Saxon work on the north wall to the Victorian porch.

Main picture: St Michael's, Upton Cressett. Over the hills west of Bridgnorth and up a quiet valley is the beautiful and remote hillside setting of this delightful, mainly Norman, church.
It is pictured here with a carpet of late-winter snowdrops.

SHROPSHIRE WILDLIFE TRUST

SHROPSHIRE Wildlife Trust cares for 37 nature reserves around the county. From ancient, mossy woods to modern, wetland bird havens, their acreage encompasses hills and valleys, flower-rich hay meadows, ancient woodlands and post-industrial spoil heaps blooming with orchids.

An open-access policy means that trust reserves can be enjoyed by people at any time, although a permit is needed for one or two of them. Guided walks take place throughout the year, from bluebell walks in spring to orchid spectaculars in summer and fungi forays in autumn.

Wildlife does not exist only on nature reserves, of course, so the trust is actively involved in promoting better countryside and green-space management all over the county. The trust works with farmers, local authorities and community groups to encourage the creation of habitats where a rich diversity of wildlife can exist.

Some species of plants and animals are in real trouble. Not long ago, lapwings bred in virtually every other field in Shropshire; today their swooping spring acrobatics are rarely seen and their wild cry seldom heard.

Their breeding numbers have plummeted, so Shropshire Wildlife Trust is working with farmers to try to reverse that trend.

The trust has many other projects, including wild-flower seed harvesting, a scheme to encourage wildlife gardening, and a project to raise awareness of the county's rich and exciting geological history. The trust also works in schools across the county to open children's eyes to the natural world and bring it close to them by creating wild areas in school grounds.

SARAH BIERLEY

Above: Marsh helleborine thriving at Sweeney Fen.

Facing page: Brook Vessons nature reserve.

Below: Tree-shaking – a school field trip.

THE CORVEDALE ON NEW YEAR'S DAY

The Swan Inn at Aston Munslow in the Corvedale is typical of the charming country inns to be found in this part of the world.

What an exhilarating start to a new year, and what an inspiring start to exploring an undiscovered county!

Always beautiful, the Corvedale is literally breathtaking when mantled by light snowfall and lit by winter sunshine from a cloudless blue sky.

When we left home at 9am on January 1, 2002 there was no snow on the ground. Half an hour later we were at the southern end of the Corvedale. For much of the morning we had the dale virtually to ourselves; most of the world was still in bed. What a shame to miss such natural beauty! The days are at their shortest at the turn of the year, of course; we knew that by three o' clock at the latest the sun would have disappeared behind the western ridges and any chance for photography would be gone.

Speed was of the essence, therefore. We slipped and slid along country lanes and up and down steep hills; plodded around churchyards in drifted snow; and drank reviving flasks of tea sitting on the back of the car. What a wonderful day we had!

The following pages show the Corvedale waking up to a new year.

BARRY FREEMAN

*Shipton Hall is one of the outstanding houses of the dale.
Built of Wenlock limestone, the house dates from the
1580s and is complemented by the Georgian stable block
with its high entrance arch and cupola, backed by a
substantial round dovecote.*

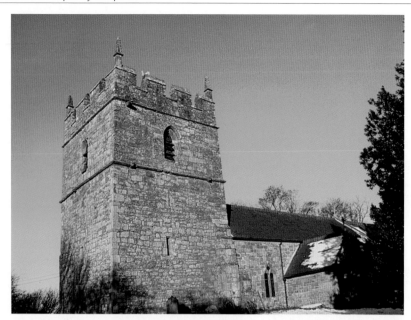

SOME CORVEDALE CHURCHES

Left: Holy Trinity at Holdgate has a Norman nave and massive stone tower. The intricately decorated doorway leads to a font with typical Norman motifs of dragon and interlaced foliage. The enjoyable woodwork includes a skilfully turned communion rail and two high-backed pews in the corner of the nave.

Below left: Heath Chapel is one of Corvedale's simplest buildings, a virtually unaltered Norman country church serving a failed medieval village. There are two other failed villages nearby: Cold Weston and Abdon.

Below: St James's church is next to Shipton Hall. Learn here the sad story of four local children, apparently illegitimate, who were sent to America on the Mayflower in 1620. Three died within months: they are now remembered in a handsome plaque on the nave wall, donated by the Massachusetts Society of Mayflower Descendants in 1996.

STANTON LONG

ONLY two miles from Holdgate, yet with a totally different architecture, this illustrates the endless variety of rural English churches. St Michael's at Stanton Long stands in a circular churchyard looking out across farmland.

There is a notable timbered roof in the nave and a good nineteenth-century reredos behind the altar.

THE STEDMANS OF CORVEDALE

THE Stedmans were a well-known Corvedale family occupying several houses in Munslow and Diddlebury parishes. This in itself would not merit special mention, were it not for the fact that the name Stedman is instantly recognisable wherever two or three bellringers are gathered together.

It was Fabian Stedman who was destined to become a legendary figure in campanology. He was born at Yarkhill, Herefordshire, in 1640, although his father was a Corvedale man: Francis Stedman was born in 1598 at the fourteenth-century White House, Aston Munslow.

Fabian Stedman's great contribution to bellringing was to devise what many ringing authorities regard as the most musical principles, or methods of change-ringing: Stedman Doubles, five bells; Triples, seven; Caters, nine; and Cinques [pronounced "sinks"], 11 bells.

For three centuries Stedman has rung throughout the land, from peals in country churches to great state occasions. In 2002, for example, at the funeral of Queen Elizabeth the Queen Mother, a peal of Stedman Caters was rung on the half-muffled bells of Westminster Abbey; a few months later at the other end of town, a joyful peal of Stedman Cinques was sung at St Paul's for the Queen's Golden Jubilee service.

Next time you hear a peal ringing over the rooftops and across the countryside, it might easily be Stedman, a man who lived three hundred years ago, from a family who arrived in the Corvedale in the 1270s.

MUNSLOW

ST Michael's enjoys an idyllic setting surrounded by yews and other evergreens, and facing down the dip slope of Wenlock Edge. The church is entered by an attractive timbered porch with decorative floor tiles, continued inside.

Immediately on the right, the first pew back is richly carved, and small carved panels decorate the ends of all the pews. From the church, a small road strikes uphill providing fine views back across the Corvedale.

Right: St Michael's, Munslow.

Opposite top: the valley above the church.

DIDDLEBURY

THE village street runs alongside a stream which has a ford as it turns to climb up to St Peter's church. The large churchyard looks down on the rooftops of the village and, from its eastern side, across the Corvedale to Brown Clee Hill.

The nave has extensive herringbone masonry on a Saxon doorway in the north wall. The building in the corner of the churchyard looks like a former village school.

Left: St Peter's, Diddlebury.

Opposite bottom: The view across the Corvedale from the churchyard.

EASTHOPE

Easthope is high up in one of the valleys, or hopes, leading up from the Corvedale on to Wenlock Edge.

The little church of St Peter, with its timbered bell turret, stands on its own in an enclosure separated from the surrounding farmland by a considerable ha-ha.

This is a remote and beautiful spot, hidden deep in the hills.

Facing page: The view from Easthope church.

CULMINGTON AND TUGFORD

At Culmington, the new open metal top to the spire at All Saints' church is a prominent landmark as one approaches the village.

At Tugford, the church of St Catherine stands by a stream and has to be approached across a field. The nave is largely unaltered Norman work. The ancient timber fittings include a fine Jacobean communion rail.

ALL Saints', Culmington, is a wonderfully light church with freshly painted white walls and immaculately maintained furnishings. The nave and chancel (opposite) are separated by a partially restored screen with a finely carved top beam.

The outward-leaning north and south walls contain restored herringbone masonry and are held in place by tie-rods meeting above the aisle.

THE SUN SETS ON NEW YEAR'S DAY . . .

Above: A view across the hills stretching south towards Clee Hill.

THE end of a bright New Year's Day in the Corvedale ends with a climb up out of the dale to seek out the remote hamlet of Abdon on the western slope of Clee Hill.

Although only mid-afternoon, the sun is setting and the temperature already below freezing. The climb is rewarded by these delightful views and the sight of the little church of St Margaret (opposite) lit by the low western sun.

Perched on an outcrop, the church overlooks the rooftops of the few scattered houses and farms in the area. Inside, visitors are rewarded with the splendid division between nave and chancel, formed from impressive timber uprights and beams.

From the church, a small road climbs on up the hill, linking the scattered houses and providing grand views across the Corvedale to Wenlock Edge.

Right: Looking up towards Brown Clee from Abdon churchyard.

ST MARGARET'S: ABDON

St Mary's Church, Bitterley

THE church stands next to Bitterley Court along a quiet byroad. Seen from the neighbouring parkland the clean, straight lines of the tower are emphasised by the brilliantly blue winter sky and snow-covered Clee Hill.

CLEE HILL

QUARRYING has scarred vast areas of Clee Hill. What we are left with today is a post-industrial landscape. Seen under snow, however, it takes on a gentler, almost lunar, appearance. Particularly when snow-covered and sunlit, Clee Hill can be seen from 50 miles away.

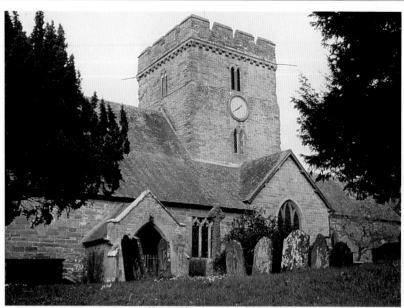

Above: The churches of Stanton Lacy and Stoke St Milborough. Below: Clee St Margaret church, interior and exterior.

❦

A Street Disguised As a Stream!

IS THIS the longest ford in England? It's about 60 yards long in Clee St Margaret, and curves around out of sight . . . certainly a surprise for any first-time motorist following the signpost to Ludlow!

A E HOUSMAN

POET AND SCHOLAR

ALFRED Edward Housman was born in 1859 and brought up close to Bromsgrove, Worcestershire, the eldest of seven children.

In 1877 he went up to St John's College, Oxford, where he made an immediate impact and appeared to have the makings of a brilliant classical scholar. Yet for one reason or another he failed to earn his honours degree, having to accept a lowlier pass degree in its place.

Being of an acutely sensitive nature, this disappointment drove him to abandon scholarly life to take up a civil service post in London, so it was with some surprise on the part of professional and personal acquaintances that his first volume of poems, *A Shropshire Lad*, was published (at his own expense) in 1896.

The collection's idealised presentation of the English countryside and the people therein led to its popularity some two decades later during the Great War – and ever since.

Housman, brother of the artist, art critic, poet and playwright Laurence Housman, died in 1936.

CLEE HILL

You and I must keep from shame
In London streets the Shropshire name;
On banks of Thames they must not say
Severn breeds worse men than they;
And friends abroad must bear in mind
Friends at home they leave behind.

Oh, I shall be stiff and cold
When I forget you, hearts of gold;
The land where I shall mind you not
Is the land where all's forgot.
And if my foot returns no more
To Teme nor Corve nor Severn shore,
Luck, my lads, be with you still
By falling stream and standing hill,
By chiming tower and whispering tree,
Men that made a man of me.

About your work in town and farm
Still you'll keep my head from harm,
Still you'll help me, hands that gave
A grasp to friend me to the grave.

From *A Shropshire Lad*

ONNY, CLUN AND TEME

THE TRANQUIL SOUTH-WEST

South-west Shropshire is the county's most sparsely populated area, an upland area of great beauty and tranquillity stretching deep into Mid Wales.

The only settlements sufficiently large to qualify as villages are found along the Clun and Teme valleys. The vast upland area between the valleys is punctuated only by tiny hamlets such as the quaintly named New Invention and isolated farmsteads.

Towards the Clun Valley from near Bettws y Crwyn.

CLUN

ALTHOUGH its military and market functions have passed into history, Clun remains an important crossing point of the River Clun, and retains an ambience of a small border town rather than a village.

The castle buildings and earthworks remain hugely impressive and provide the best vantage points for dramatic views of the town and the surrounding hilly countryside.

Trinity Hospital is a quadrangle of early-seventeenth-century almshouses with an additional mid-nineteenth-century wing and a chapel with box pews. The garden has two lifelike cast figures of elderly almsmen.

The medieval bridge is narrow, with pedestrian refuges in the parapets of the cutwaters. Adjacent is a former temperance hall, a reminder of the days when Clun supported some 15 inns and drinking houses.

Facing page (clockwise from top): Clun Castle and ditches; a view over the town from the castle; the almshouses; and Clun bridge.

THE CLUN VALLEY

THE UPPER CLUN

NEWCASTLE was a small defensive point at a crossing of the River Clun on the line of Offa's Dyke. The church of St John Evangelist has an extremely unusual pivotal lych gate (facing page, top left).

Determination is needed to locate the remote little church of Bettws y Crwyn (facing page), high in the hills between the valleys of Clun and Teme. There is impressive woodwork, particularly in the nave roof and the superbly carved rood screen. The unique feature is the painted names of parish farms on the pew-ends.

THE MIDDLE CLUN

Clunbury is the location for the two views on this page. Here the valley widens at its junction with the River Kemp. At most times of the year, the Clun is a placid river; the scene below looks downstream from Clunbury bridge.

From the bridge the road climbs up the valley side, where attractive houses and farm buildings cluster around the church of St Swithun (below left).

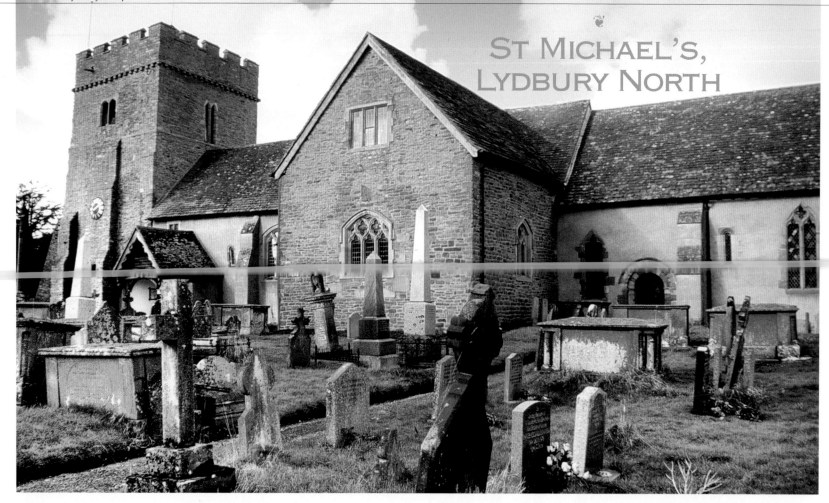

St Michael's, Lydbury North

THIS is a small village which boasts a large church, impressive from the road, with two quite large transepts as well as a substantial nave, chancel and tower.

Inside, one is immediately impressed by the large painted commandments and creed which are displayed above the screen.

The transepts house two chapels: the Walcot in the south transept, the Plowden in the north. These are named after the two big houses in the parish. Walcot Hall lies across the valley from the village, looking out across a long lake created by damming the River Kemp. This was the home of Clive of India, built on his instructions in the 1760s. Plowden Hall lies up a side valley east of the village, a timber-framed house in the possession of the same family for eight centuries.

St Cuthbert's, Clungunford

LOCATED at the western extremity of the village, Clungunford's church of St Cuthbert looks across meadows to the Clun meandering peacefully southwards to its confluence with the Teme, just across the Herefordshire border. This is a delightful spot to encounter in the sunshine of a bright February morning.

The features are particularly memorable: the impressive size of the chancel, which is the same height as the nave and separated only by a simple arch, giving a remarkably spacious impression to the whole interior; and the positioning of the tower of 1895 on the north side of the nave, an unusual configuration necessitated by the space limitations of St Cuthbert's raised site at its western end.

HOPTON CASTLE

THE castle guarded a route between the Clun and Teme valleys. The Norman keep still stands, surrounded by earthworks which indicate the more extensive area the fortifications once encompassed. The site lacks any relief features which could have aided defence, and the castle ended its military role in the Civil War.

In 1644, a small force of Parliamentarians withstood a Royalist seige for three weeks before surrendering on apparently agreed terms. However, all except their commander were brutally killed and it is recorded that the term "Hopton quarter" was coined for any particularly savage act of treachery.

HOPESAY

"THE heart of south Shropshire" proclaims a plaque on a seat in the main street, and this is just how it feels.

Hopesay is a tranquil village surrounded by high hills. Most of the houses are set discreetly back from the road in tree-filled gardens and grounds. Particularly memorable is the number of towering wellingtonia in the village centre.

At the right time of year, a carpet of snowdrops provides a delightful introduction to the church of St Mary (below). Inside, the nave provides a feast of enjoyable features: the patterned ceiling; the west gallery and fine pews; the three double-light stained-glass windows in the south wall; and, particularly striking, the tall north-wall memorial of twin figures set in mosaic with marble surround, dating to 1901–02.

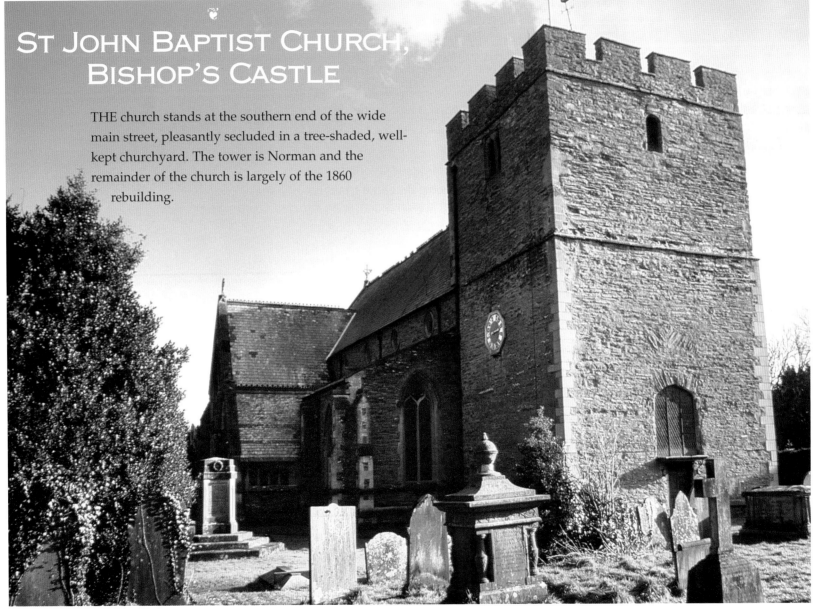

St John Baptist Church, Bishop's Castle

THE church stands at the southern end of the wide main street, pleasantly secluded in a tree-shaded, well-kept churchyard. The tower is Norman and the remainder of the church is largely of the 1860 rebuilding.

BISHOP'S CASTLE

FORTUNATELY, the main road bypasses the historic town centre, allowing it to be itself; a bustling little local centre crowded on the slope below the former castle site. Inevitably, it has developed as the main tourist magnet for the area: it is a picturesque, constantly entertaining town with surprises in every street.

The castle was built on a commanding site overlooking a broad valley, by the bishops of Hereford. The story runs that the Anglo-Saxon lord of the manor of Lydbury North, one Egwin Shakehead, was cured of an affliction at the shrine of St Ethelbert in Hereford cathedral. In gratitude, he bequeathed his manor to the bishops and they built a castle.

A small town of classic layout developed, with a street running downhill from the castle to a church at the far end. Alleys branched off and, in the middle of the eighteenth century, a smart new town hall was built across the top end of the main street. This today is the dominant building as one ascends the street; of the castle which once towered above the rooftops, virtually nothing remains.

Bishop's Castle richly rewards leisurely exploration. Steep little streets and individually designed buildings, both shops and houses, are all crowded together on the hillside: an essential contribution to the historic aspect of the spirit of Shropshire.

Left: The view north along the main street through the lych gate.
Right: The town's "house on stilts" and a picture from the past.

Bishop's Castle Town Hall.

Above: The Porch House in Bishop's Castle.
Below: An aerial view of the town.

STOWE is a remote hamlet up a side valley. St Michael's church stands among conifers and yews, apparently little changed for centuries, with ancient stone walls and a splendid timbered roof. The rough stone lane is more watercourse than thoroughfare.

THE TEME VALLEY

THE Teme flows in a narrower, more steep-sided valley than the Clun, following a parallel course eastwards from Wales into England. For some distance it forms the southern county boundary between Shropshire and Wales.

Pictured below is a classic winter scene.

BUCKNELL is a large village with various attractive areas, especially around St Mary's church. It stands in a raised, well-maintained churchyard. Inside, massive timbers support the bell frame.

Beyond the church, the village street leads down to the River Redlake, past the Old School House with the sign on the door: "Beware of the Rod"!

Llanfair Waterdine has an impressive display of embroidered hassocks. The Teme Valley is narrow and steep-sided here, where another remote, beautiful hidden valley, Cwm Collo, dips down to the Teme.

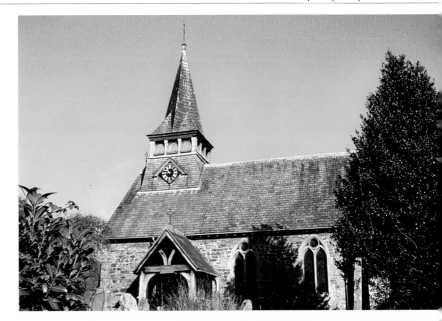

Top: St Mary's church, Bucknell.
Right: Interior of the church of St Mary, Llanfair Waterdine.

BEDSTONE

THE first site of Bedstone Court (below) is quite breathtaking. Situated in beautifully maintained parkland, this is Victorian timber framing at its most impressive. Built in 1884 and now owned by Bedstone College, this is a rare example of a "calendar house": 365 windows, 52 rooms and 12 chimneys. There is a superb stained-glass window depicting the months above the main staircase.

Left: St Mary's church on the hillside above Bucknell.
Below: Bedstone Court now has an educational role.

THE RECRUIT

LEAVE YOUR HOME BEHIND, LAD,

AND REACH YOUR FRIENDS YOUR HAND,

AND GO, AND LUCK GO WITH YOU

WHILE LUDLOW TOWER SHALL STAND.

OH, COME YOU HOME OF SUNDAY

WHEN LUDLOW STREETS ARE STILL

AND LUDLOW BELLS ARE CALLING

TO FARM AND LANE AND MILL,

OR COME YOU HOME OF MONDAY

WHEN LUDLOW MARKET HUMS

AND LUDLOW CHIMES ARE PLAYING

"THE CONQUERING HERO COMES."

From Housman's A Shropshire Lad

FROM TEME TO SEVERN

This is the hilly undulating country that comprises the south-eastern corner of the county; a land of small villages hidden in valleys and reached by a network of minor roads, often requiring some fairly alert navigation!

It is the land between the prominent landmark of Clee Hill and the Wyre Forest, where Shropshire quietly merges into neighbouring Worcestershire.

Ludlow is the obvious place to start. The following pages show a selection of nooks and corners of one of England's most important small towns – a major element not just of the spirit of Shropshire, but of the spirit of England itself.

LUDLOW

AS at Shrewsbury, the Normans selected a naturally defensible site, placing castle and town on a spur dropping steeply on three sides to the Teme and the Corve. The steep valley sides of the Teme and the flood plain of the Corve have subsequently deterred expansion of the town in all directions except eastwards.

Today, therefore, if you approach Ludlow across either of the Teme bridges you have the rare delight of entering immediately the historic core of the town. The latest buildings passed are Georgian. Almost the same is true of the approach from the north across the Corve.

Ludlow is a delightful town: the great triumvirate of twentieth-century authorities, Pevsner, Betjemen and Clifton-Taylor, all sang its praises – and justifiably so. It was a planned Norman town, set down to secure the western boundaries of newly conquered

Facing page: Features of St Laurence's Church in Ludlow include the east window, intricately carved misericords and a stone memorial.

This page: An example of fine timber framing (top), and the regular Ludlow market which takes place in Castle Square.

territory. The historic core is small and easy to comprehend.

The castle was positioned at the western end, using the near-vertical cliffs to deter attack. A large outer bailey was walled, providing a defensible space sufficiently large to accommodate substantial numbers of armed men and civilians. A broad street-cum-market area stretched eastwards to the church. In medieval times, the eastern length of the street was filled with closely packed rows of timber-framed townhouses, providing a fascinating series of parallel alleys.

The demolition of the Victorian Market Hall in the 1980s opened up the area outside the castle gate again, and gave a proper sense of space to the western end of the main street.

Delights abound everywhere in Ludlow: the church of St Laurence; the splendid streets, alleys and courtyards; scores of medieval and Georgian buildings and, of course, the castle.

Ludlow is a town crucial not just to the spirit of Shropshire but to the whole fabric of English townscapes. Long may it remain so.

Left: A bridge over the River Teme.

Above: The town's Buttermarket.

Above right: Ludlow racecourse.

Right: The Gate House at Bromfield.

The Norman chapel below sits inside the inner wall (main picture).

ST MARY: CAYNHAM

NEEN SOLLARS: CONYNGESBY'S MONUMENT

ALL SAINTS: NEEN SOLLARS

THE wooden lych gate remembers the local men sacrificed in the Great War. A long path leads through a grove of yews dotted with ancient tombstones. The church retains an ancient look despite extensive rebuilding in 1885. The preaching cross has withstood the weather of many centuries, and is an important element of the local heritage.

HUMFREY Conyngesby died in 1624. His monument in the south transept is the outstanding feature of Neen Sollars church. The monument is alabaster and of good quality in all its parts, including the detailed inscriptions.

THIS is an impressive cruciform church with a massive central tower, all built in sandstone and little altered since its building in the late thirteenth century.

The church dominates the small village, which is located on the steeply sloping western side of the River Rea, a tributary of the Teme.

ST MARY: ASHFORD CARBONEL

ST MARY: INTERIOR

ST ANDREW: ASHFORD BOWDLER

THE church is on the edge of the village with a memorable view across a farming landscape of wide fields to Clee Hill. The well-kept churchyard is shaded by grand yews.

There is an unusual iron tomb chest (1806) in the south-east corner.

THE picture shows the church decorated for Christmas. The beams are very impressive, right through from belfry to chancel.

The east window arrangement is unusual, comprising two narrow lancets and an oval vessica.

ASHFORD Bowdler is immediately across the Teme from Ashford Carbonel. St Andrew's church is located right on the bank of this capricious river, above a sheer 20-foot drop. In 1906, following work which was intended to underpin the east end, the whole chancel collapsed into the river. The 1907 rebuilding accurately recreated the Norman chancel.

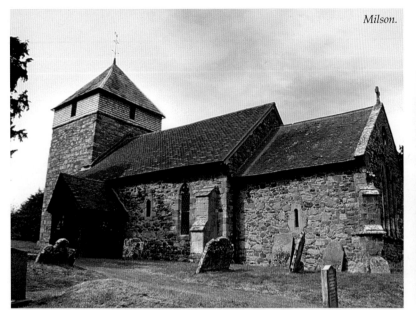

Milson.

Neen S

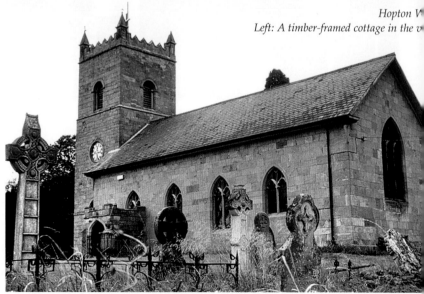

Hopton W
Left: A timber-framed cottage in the v

In The Peaceful Hills

EXPLORING the little-frequented byroads, often between high banks, one encounters myriad villages and hamlets, all with their own special character and delightful churches.

The church of St George, Milson, remains largely Norman, hidden behind trees beside a small village green.

At Neen Savage, St Mary's stands above the River Rea; the road dips steeply down and crosses the river through a ford.

At Hopton Wafers, the village is between Hopton Court and the main Cleobury Mortimer road. St Michael's faces a row of attractive cottages.

Throughout this district, one encounters views of Clee Hill, pictured above right under a layer of snow.

The church shown right is that at Hope Bagot, in a secluded valley setting on the southern flank of Clee Hill. The church of St John Baptist makes a delightful group along with the neighbouring cottages, village hall and tumbling stream.

Just east of Nash stands this mighty oak (above), gnarled and battered from defying the storms of centuries. Across the road, a fine Georgian house (opposite) looks out over its lawn and a beautiful green pool. Beside the pool are apple trees, laden with fruit.

CORELEY AND NASH

CORELEY is a scattered hamlet east of Clee Hill. St Peter's church (above left) stands alone in rolling farmland. The stone tower is thirteenth century; the brick nave and chancel mid-eighteenth century.

At Nash, the church of St John Baptist stands between Nash Court and the former village school. The eighteenth-century court is pictured (left) across farmland from the church.

BURFORD

THE village of Burford takes its name from the river crossing that was the site of a fortified Roman settlement. Indeed it is only the river that separates the village from Tenbury Wells and Worcestershire.

The church of St Mary stands apart from the village, and inside, the church's history is apparent, particularly in the many fine tombs to the Cornwall family who were lords of Burford for around four centuries.

Burford House, an early Georgian gentleman's residence, has magnificent gardens and is now home to Burford House Garden Centre, home of the national Clematis collection.

Above: A wildflower meadow at Burford.

Left: Burford House holds the national Clematis collection, involving hundreds of varieties.

Right: The church of St Mary seen from the Burford House gardens.

The reredos in St Mary's, Burford.

CLEOBURY MORTIMER

CLEOBURY Mortimer is less a small town than a large village, but it has a complex industrial past: in particular, its fulling mills were of importance, as was its wood industry. Being on the slopes of Titterstone Clee, minerals such as coal and iron were available. Later industries included paper-making as well as mining.

At the time of the Norman Conquest, Cleobury Mortimer was held by the wife of Edward the Confessor; afterwards by Ralph de Mortimer, who gave his name to the town

The magnificent Church of the Virgin has a wonderfully crooked spire, the result of its oak beams warped by wind, rain and time.

Cleobury is believed to be the birthplace in the fourteenth century of William Langland, the author of *Piers Plowman*. John Betjeman described it as "A long, airy curving street of brick Georgian houses and shops interspersed with genuine half-timber, the Rea brook making a splash at the bottom of the hill. The whole church seems to have slipped out of shape".

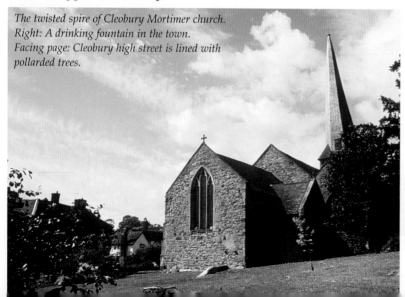

The twisted spire of Cleobury Mortimer church.
Right: A drinking fountain in the town.
Facing page: Cleobury high street is lined with pollarded trees.

Above: St Peter's, Chelmarsh stands in a carefully maintained churchyard. The brick tower of 1720 is framed by yews flanking the approach path.

Top right: St John Baptist in Ditton Priors makes a delightful centrepiece for the village, together with the Howard Arms inn and neighbouring houses.

Right: Burwarton Park before 7 o'clock on a spring morning. The village ambience is greatly enhanced by the extensive parkland setting.

ON A MAY EVENING . . .

THESE pictures were taken as a perfect spring day drew to a close, high up on Titterstone Clee Hill. At Cleeton St Mary (left) the Pardoe Almshouses face the village green and church.

Lower down, tucked away in hidden valleys are St Mary's church in the attractive village of Stottesdon (below) and St Giles's in the lovely little village of Farlow.

AROUND BRIDGNORTH AND MUCH WENLOCK

QUATFORD (below left) is located along the base of the red sandstone cliffs which form the eastern side of the Severn Valley, south of Bridgnorth.

At Quatt, the red brick tower and nave (left) are of 1763, giving the church of St Andrew a clearly Georgian appearance. But the chancel and north side of the church are equally clearly medieval.

St Mary's church at Alveley (below) is tucked away at one end of the extensive village in a sunny spot overlooking the Severn. The approach to the church is flanked by some extremely enjoyable and well-maintained older houses.

THE RIVERSIDE IN SPRING

FIND yourself in the right place at the right time . . . These delightful springtime scenes were recorded in the Severn Valley at Highley and Hampton Loade in the vicinity of the two railway stations. The footpath (below) was heavy with the aroma of wild garlic after a heavy shower.

CONSERVATION IN ACTION

WE should all be grateful to those who spend countless hours keeping alive our technical heritage in all its forms. Here in Shropshire there are the Severn Valley Railway and Daniel's Mill side by side to remind us of the way things were.

On the facing page are three scenes from Highley: the interior of the signal box with the signalman stoking his fire; changing tokens so that the train can proceed beyond the station; and 7802 Bradley Manor standing at the platform with an up-train to Bridgnorth. The fourth picture shows Hampton Loade station with its nostalgic advertisements for life's little necessities.

Daniel's Mill (right) has England's largest waterwheel still powering a corn mill. It ceased working in 1957 but has since been painstakingly restored by the miller's son, using authentic materials from demolished properties. Installed around 1855, the wheel is 38 feet in diameter. It was necessary to construct it this large to fully utilise the power of the small stream running down to the Severn.

❦
BRIDGNORTH

CONTINUING the theme of the preceding pages, it is still possible to arrive at Bridgnorth by steam railway, at the station which is maintained just as it was in the heyday of steam travel. The grand footbridge (left) is dated 1887 and still has its proud GWR insignia.

The Cliff Railway (below left) is yet another aspect of our technical heritage being conserved in full working order. Such is the drop between the town centre and the riverside that this railway remains as important in the 21st century as it was to its first Victorian passengers.

The gardens (facing page) are one of Bridgnorth's most delightful areas, with a promenade and viewpoint across the valley to the surrounding countryside. The only part of the once-extensive castle remaining is the lower stage of the keep, leaning at an angle far more acute than the much more widely known tower at Pisa. Behind it rises the dome of Telford's church of St Mary Magdalene, built in the 1790s.

❦

ASPECTS OF BRIDGNORTH

NUMEROUS fascinating medieval alleys crowd the historic centre of the town, lined with a variety of building styles. Church Street ascends to Victorian St Leonard's church standing in an open churchyard like a small cathedral close. The Churches Conservation Trust (see page 33) cares for St Leonard's.

The town hall dates from 1652, with timber-framed upper chambers and brick-faced stone for the arched open market area below.

Facing page, clockwise from top left:
North Gate was wholly restored in 1910, providing a clear division between the High Street and the suburbs.

The interior of the church of St Mary Magdalene is a wonderfully light and airy space; the apse was added in 1876.

A view down to the Severn from the terrace of St Mary Magdalene, showing the 1823 bridge.

The Italianate brick-built New Market, built in blue, yellow and red brick was constructed in 1855 and dominates the southern end of the High Street.

BOXING DAY IN BRIDGNORTH

NO Dickensian white Christmas for Bridgnorth! These pictures show the town at midday on Boxing Day 2002, and people are having to shield their eyes against the brightness of the sun shining from a Mediterranean sky. The town is crowded and many shops are open, along with hostelries and eating houses.

The broad High Street has fortunately been retained from its Norman origins, not subdivided by later alleys as at Ludlow. The construction of the town hall (right) has provided added interest, not a barrier, because the high, arched openings allow the eye to pass through to North Gate at the upper end of the street.

It would be difficult to imagine a main street with a greater variety of building styles in a town of this modest size. The timber-framed Swan Inn (below right) is a prime example, flanked by smaller timber buildings followed by Georgian brick facades.

For its dramatic site and wonderful array of streets, alleys and buildings, Bridgnorth is a gem of a town which amply repays leisurely exploration.

The Severn Valley Railway at Oldbury Viaduct.

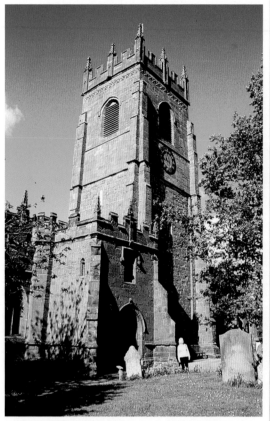

CLAVERLEY: ALL SAINTS

MONUMENTS AT CLAVERLEY

WORFIELD: ST PETER'S

A LARGE, imposing church in the centre of the village, the tower soars over the rooftops at the top of the hill on which this attractive village stands. Simon Jenkins rates this as a three-star church in his *England's Thousand Best Churches*. The medieval murals are a treasure of national significance.

THERE are a number of well-executed monuments in All Saints, including the incised tomb cover illustrated above. Francis Gateacre was an Elizabethan whose estate (now Gatacre) was some three miles south of Claverley. The incised slabs are particularly interesting for the clarity of their inscriptions and the costume details they provide.

A SLENDER spire provides a landmark as one approaches the village. Like its neighbour in Claverley it glows rich red in the sunshine and is full of good things inside: notice particularly the screen and the impressive east window beyond, and the splendid Bromley late sixteenth- and early seventeenth-century monuments.

CLAVERLEY AND WORFIELD

THESE are two neighbouring and very attractive villages east of Bridgnorth.

Below is shown a part of the wall paintings in Claverley church dating from around 1200 and presumed to depict the battle between the Virtues and the Vices. The sequence runs the length of the north wall of the nave, some 50 feet.

Right is the picturesque timber-framed vicarage at the entrance to Claverley's well-kept churchyard.

Below right is the street approaching Worfield church. It is lined with attractive cottages in a variety of styles.

P G WODEHOUSE

"PLUM"

"LET'S tootle down to Shropshire, Jeeves!" Bertie Wooster would exclaim on the rare occasions when he felt moved to briefly desert the metropolis and his cronies at the Drones Club.

Off they would go in the old two-seater with the hood down – the sun usually shone in that halcyon world created by PGW; a world inhabited by an endearing cast of winsome maidens, formidable aunts and barmy aristocrats, who kept us laughing from the mid-twenties onwards.

Wodehouse lived at Hays House, Stableford, and spent the holidays in the placid setting of turn-of-the-century rural Shropshire. Those few years remained in his memory for the rest of his long life, doubtless taking on an ever-rosier hue viewed from his rather sad, exiled life in America. Here was set Blandings Castle, inhabited by Lord Emsworth, constantly beleaguered by his extraordinary family and fortunately able to find solace and contentment in the company of his prize sow, The Empress of Blandings.

As with Housman, Shropshire represented the archetypal rural idyll for Wodehouse. In both it inspired some of the twentieth century's most memorable writing.

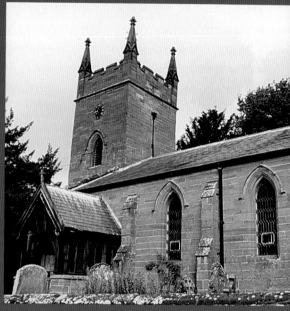

Badger's church of St Giles; this village became Badgerwick in Wodehouse's novels. It is the church nearest to Stableford.

> *"I have often felt that life at Blandings must have been a very pleasant affair, if not for Lord Emsworth and his pig, at any rate for visitors to the castle. Plenty of ridin', shootin' and fishin' for the sportively inclined, and the browsing and sluicing of course beyond criticism. I have always refrained from describing the meals there, not wishing to make my readers' mouths water excessively, but I can now divulge that they were of the best and rendered all the more toothsome by being presided over by butler Beach, who also never failed to bring the tray of beverages into the drawing room at 9.30.*
>
> *"The one thing that might be considered to militate against the peace of life at Blandings was the constant incursion of impostors . . . Without at least one impostor on the premises, Blandings Castle is never itself."*
>
> **Preface to *Something Fresh***

MUCH WENLOCK

THE church precincts are more park than churchyard.
This picture shows the buildings backing on to the park,
including the timbered Guildhall of 1540. Across the
park are the remains of Wenlock Priory
(see page 30).

❦

A LOCAL AFFAIR

WHAT a difference some flowers make! The cottage doorways (above left) in the Bull Ring make a delightful introduction to one of the main streets.

The shops in the town are locally owned; no facades of the national multiples spoil the sense of a friendly traditional town.

Inside the church, the tapestry (above) catches the eye: it was worked by Lady Gaskell in the early twentieth century and is a copy of some Burne-Jones designs for the Morris Company.

IN THE SUNSHINE

THE fine timber-framed building (below) is dated 1682 and carries the names of John and Mary Raynalds. On the right are two views of the town centre showing the Jubilee fountain and clock tower; the Agricultural Library of 1852; the Guildhall; and the tower of Holy Trinity church.

How fortunate that the main roads are diverted away from the town centre, allowing this delightful little town to exist at peace.

THE STRETTONS AND THEIR HILLS

One can well envy the first-time visitor by road or rail who enters the Church Stretton valley and sees, almost unbelievingly, the great bulks of Caer Caradoc and the Lawley rising almost sheer from the valley floor.

ON THE LONG MYND

THE thin, acid soils on the long mynd (right) support a cover of heather, bracken and tussocky grassland which, together with the deeply incised valleys, provide habitats for birds of prey, bog plants and insects. The streams support a wide range of invertebrates which in turn feed fish and dippers. High above, raven, curlew and buzzard are a common sight.

Facing page: A view north-eastwards from the Long Mynd showing the majestic procession of Caer Caradoc (1,492 feet), then the Lawley (1,225 feet) and, across the Severn in the distance, the Wrekin (1,323 feet). In the far distance can be glimpsed wooded Hoar Edge and Wenlock Edge, flanking the upper end of Ape Dale.

RAGLETH HILL

RAGLETH (left) is the southernmost of three great hills, where the valley narrows sharply. This view looks across from near Little Stretton on a cloudless day in January. It is early afternoon but the sun is already sinking behind the Long Mynd, throwing the undulations of the lower slopes into sharp relief.

Ragleth rises to almost 1,300 feet.

THE STRETTON CHURCHES

THE three churches of the Strettons reflect the expansion of the valley's popularity in the second half of the nineteenth century after the coming of the railways.

Church Stretton was marketed as "Little Switzerland in England" and enjoyed considerable popularity from 1880 onwards. The two churches shown on this page were built as daughter churches to the long-established main church at Church Stretton.

Left: St Michael and All Angels at All Stretton (1902) is stone-built and is shared with the local United Reformed Church congregation.

Below: All Saints at Little Stretton (1903) was originally iron-roofed but the noise of the rain rendered the priest inaudible, so it was provided with a thatched roof – originally heather off the Long Mynd but then straw.

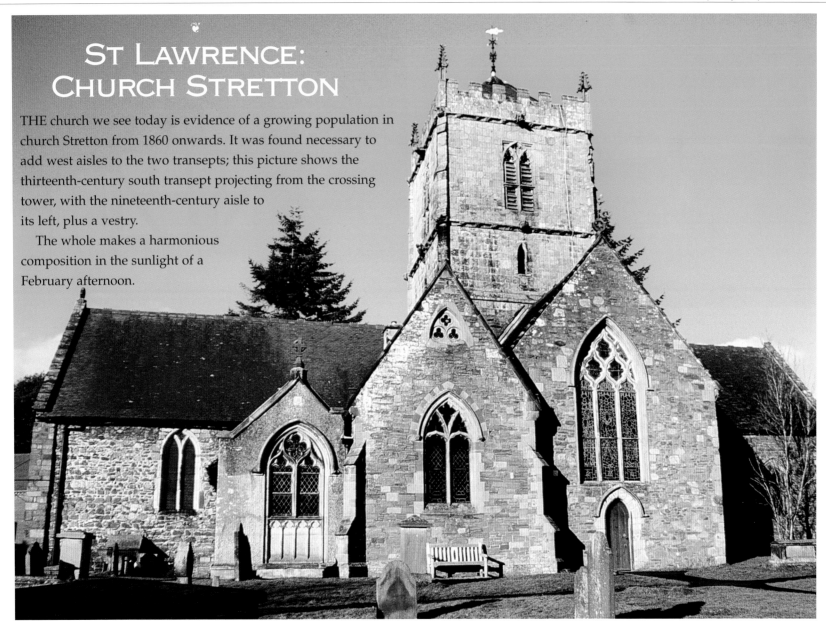

St Lawrence: Church Stretton

THE church we see today is evidence of a growing population in church Stretton from 1860 onwards. It was found necessary to add west aisles to the two transepts; this picture shows the thirteenth-century south transept projecting from the crossing tower, with the nineteenth-century aisle to its left, plus a vestry.

The whole makes a harmonious composition in the sunlight of a February afternoon.

Above: Minton is a group of cottages and smallholdings around a village green – a settlement pattern that has survived virtually unaltered from pre-Norman times.

Right: This cottage by a ford just outside Little Stretton could be a detail from a Constable painting.

Facing page: A lovely spot: the little road climbing up in the hills towards Minton, giving increasingly extensive views into the valley below.

❦

INTO THE HILLS

ON a1 classic spring evening, take a drive out of Little Stretton and up into the hills to the remote hamlet of Minton. There are some deeply appealing scenes to be discovered. . .

MALCOLM SAVILLE

LONG LIVE THE LONE PINE CLUB!

MALCOLM Saville was one of the most popular and prolific writers of children's adventure stories of the twentieth century.

Sales of his books exceed three million, and countless adults who grew up with Children's Hour will recall the gripping serials adapted from a number of his adventures.

Saville finds a place in the *Spirit of Shropshire* because it was the hills and valleys of the area around Church Stretton that provided the inspiration and setting for many of his books – especially those featuring the Lone Pine Club.

A native of Winchelsea in Sussex, Malcolm Saville discovered the south Shropshire hills in the 1930s, and his wife and children were evacuated there in 1941. Although fond of Sussex, he became entranced with the Clees, the Long Mynd and the black Stiperstones; they were "a solace and an inspiration," and Saville credited them with "any modest success I have achieved as a writer".

Unlike Housman, Malcolm Saville knew his Shropshire hills landscape intimately, although he changed the names of all the places. This enchanting landscape worked its magic on him and literally millions of children – many now approaching their seventies – will always be grateful for that.

The Stiperstones.

Two views from Eastridge, south-west of Pontesbury. Above left: Looking west over Minsterley and the Rea Brook valley to Aston Hill. Left: The landscape east near Habberley, with Lawn Hill in the background.

Above: The Darnford Brook which rises on Wild Moor and flows down through Ratlinghope to join the East Onny. Below: A view of the East Onny valley from Stedment.

CRAVEN ARMS

THE Roman Watling Street West came through here, and over the centuries the town grew up as a market centre at the junction of roads converging from all directions and heading into Mid Wales; it was a borderlands meeting point.

When the railways arrived, with the junction of the Mid Wales line right down to South Wales, Craven Arms expanded substantially. What we see today therefore is essentially a Victorian town with earlier survivals.

Pictured here are (left) the neo-Tudor school and public house, with the recent addition of a sign for the Secret Hills Discovery Centre visitor attraction; a parade of Victorian shops (below left); and (below) the Old Rectory at Stokesay, which has now become a southern extension of Craven Arms.

Above: Rushbury is a delightful village in Ape Dale, grouped around St Peter's church and overlooked by Wenlock Edge.

Left: In the grounds of the manor house at Church Preen this ancient yew is reputed to be the oldest tree in Europe.

Above right: The little church of St John Baptist at Hughley was mistakenly provided with a steeple by Housman in A Shropshire Lad. In reality it is crowned with this attractive timber-and-brick bellcote.

Right: At Monkhopton, St Peter's church has ancient features. The tower was added in an 1835 restoration.

The impressive sixteenth-century house (above) is at the southern entrance to Cardington where the road drops down from Cardington Hill.

Snailbeach is a famous lead-mining area on the northern flank of the Stiperstones ridge. The village (above left) is backed by the ridge; the main mine area (left) is a treasure trove for industrial archaeologists.

St Mary's church at Westbury (right) has a tower of 1735 and is well endowed with windows from the 1878 restoration.

COUNTRY CHURCHES OF WEST SHROPSHIRE

ST MICHAEL: CHIRBURY

THE church, dedicated to St Michael, is impressive, and its size is explained by its connection with Chirbury Priory. It is very ancient, having been restored by Humphrey de Winsbury in 1127.

ST PETER: MORE

A HAMLET church in the flat landscape between the hills of the Welsh border. It was built in 1845 and has been little touched since.

ALL SAINTS: WORTHEN

A MEDIEVAL church with a fine spacious nave and a brick chancel of 1761.

❦

MARY WEBB

AN AUTHOR WHO BELATEDLY GAINED THE RECOGNITION SHE DESERVES

FOR her devotees, Mary Webb is the essential Shropshire novelist and poet.

Her novels were all set in a countryside that remains largely as she knew it, especially when one ventures away from the main settlements and roads and on to the slopes of Lyth Hill and Pontesford Hill, or further south-west into the tranquil borderlands of the county.

Mary's parents were George and Sarah Meredith of Leighton, south-east of Shrewsbury. In her childhood she developed the twin characteristics which were to stand her in such good stead in later life: an intimate familiarity with the countryside and a love of writing. She was the eldest of six children and wrote plays and stories for her brothers and sisters.

Tragedy struck when Mary was afflicted with a thyroid disorder which left her disfigured and self-conscious to the extent that she retreated into a solitary world, concentrating on poetry and nature writing. Despite this, however, she met and married a teacher, Henry Webb, in 1912 and moved with

him to Weston-super-Mare.

Mary could not settle away from Shropshire and they returned, with Henry obtaining a teaching post at the Priory School in Shrewsbury. They had a small bungalow built at Lyth Hill, where Mary spent probably the happiest part of her life. Her earliest works were collected and published as *The Spring of Joy* in 1917, followed by *The House in Dormer Forest* in 1920.

Mary was gaining little recognition in the literary world, however, and once again the Webbs left Shropshire, this time for London. *Seven for a Secret*, set in south-west Shropshire, was completed and published in 1922, and two years later her most popular novel, *Precious Bane*. Some recognition came from the literary world now, but this enthusiasm was not reflected in sales to the general public.

By 1927 Mary Webb's health, irreparably damaged by her thyroid trouble, was deteriorating rapidly. Her marriage had failed too and she returned to Shropshire alone; she died on a visit to St Leonard's on Sea.

Now, more than 75 years later, Mary Webb continues to be read and remembered. There is a flourishing Mary Webb Society with a worldwide membership.

Facing page (clockwise from top left):
The Old Post Office at Leighton in the Severn Valley,
upstream from Buildwas.

The imposing tower of St George's church at Pontesbury.

Horses grazing peacefully on the slope of Pontesford Hill.

WILFRED OWEN

"ABOVE ALL I AM NOT CONCERNED WITH POETRY; MY SUBJECT IS WAR AND THE PITY OF WAR. THE POETRY IS IN THE PITY."

WILFRED Owen, along with Sassoon and Brooke, was a leading member of the generation of poets that experienced front-line conditions in the Great War.

His best-known works have found a secure place in the national archive of the twentieth century, and will speak to mankind of its folly for as long as people continue to read and listen to poetry.

A native of Oswestry, Owen moved to Birkenhead with his family at the age of four, but they returned to Shrewsbury ten years later in 1907. He attended the Technical College, studying assiduously for admission to London University, but was forced to take up employment in a Shrewsbury elementary school because he lacked the funds to support a university course.

After a period in which he suffered other reverses he became tutor to a French family in the Pyrenees, where he had more time to study and write poetry. But in 1915 he returned home and enlisted, being commissioned into the Manchester Regiment.

Posted to France in 1916, he quickly matured, coming to regard war with horror and disgust, and as the supreme crime against humanity.

Owen survived several traumatic incidents, but developed shell-shock and was repatriated to hospital in Scotland where he encountered Siegfried Sassoon, who encouraged and influenced his poetic writings. By August 1918 he was back in France, however, still writing poetry during lulls in the fighting. Only four of his poems were published in his lifetime.

Owen was killed on November 4, 1918, one week before the armistice was signed. News of his death reached Shrewsbury on November 11 at the same time as news of the end of the Great War was filtering through.

Holy Trinity church, Uffington: Wilfred Owen worshipped here on summer Sundays with his parents when they lived in Shrewsbury. They would cross the nearby River Severn by ferry.

Shall they return to beatings of great bells
In wild train-loads?
A few, a few, too few for drums and yells,
May creep back, silent, to still village wells
Up half-known roads.

From The Send-off

EXPLORING AROUND SHREWSBURY

CRONKHILL (right) sits across the Severn from Attingham Park. Regarded as the first Italianate house ever built in England, it was constructed for the agent of the Attingham estate. The original, white-painted house consisted of two towers joined by an L-shaped wing with a projecting balcony and colonnade.

Albright Hussey (below right) is a fascinating former moated house (part of the moat is seen in the foreground). The timber-framed part belongs to the 1520s; the brick-and-stone extension to 1601. The two contrasting styles combine to make a memorable composition . . . something planners would never allow today! Visitors should watch out for swans on the moat with their feathery, black plumage.

TWO OF SHROPSHIRE'S GRANDEST HOUSES

CONDOVER Hall (above) is Shropshire's grandest Elizabethan mansion, completed around 1600 and built of light-red sandstone.

Pitchford Hall, meanwhile, (right) was about 30 years earlier and still in the timber-framed tradition. It is the county's prime example. The multi-gabled ornate facade is seen to best effect looking down the long valley of parkland from the south.

Left: Condover church has a remarkable collection of monuments. Shown is G F Watts's striking kneeling figure of Sir Thomas Cholmondeley (d. 1864) and, behind, a four-figure wall monument from the 1640s.

ACTON BURNELL

THE castle of Acton Burnell is of national importance and in the care of English Heritage. It is in fact a fortified house rather than a castle for serious defence, and was built for Robert Burnell, Lord Chancellor and Bishop of Bath and Wells.

He obtained his licence to crenellate in 1284 and was allowed to use timber from the royal forests.

The quality of workmanship still evident in the castle clearly indicates that Burnell was able to employ the most up-to-date architectural craftsmen, and a similar situation is evidenced in the nearby church.

St Mary was certainly provided with the latest in thirteenth-century designs, but had no tower until the 1880s, when a low, fairly modest one was erected in the angle between the north transept and chancel.

Castle and church are set away from the main village streets, which contain a variety of attractive houses. The minor road leading due south rises steadily along the edge of Park Wood and provides a fine view of the south Shropshire hills.

Top: Acton Burnell church.
Right: The view looking towards the Lawley in the
direction of Church Stretton.

Left: Acton Burnell Castle was a fortified manor house rather than a true castle.

Below left: Langley, to the south of Acton Burnell, has a fascinating gatehouse – timber-framed one side, stone the other. Langley Hall itself has been demolished.

Below: Langley Chapel dates from around 1600, standing on its own and in the care of English Heritage.

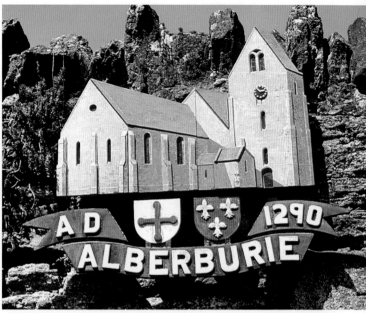

At Baschurch (above) the large red sandstone church of All Saints stands in neatly maintained surroundings in a quiet corner of this busy village. The tower remains largely thirteenth century, clearly a different-coloured sandstone from the renewed chancel and nave.

Ruyton-XI-Towns is built along the upper slope of a valley looking out over the River Perry. The church of St John Baptist (below) is also of red sandstone with a Norman nave and chancel.

At Alberbury the castle ruins (below) are very much in evidence, close to St Michael's church. The village sign (above) has been carefully crafted to show this unusual church.

Above: The Georgian bridge across the Severn at Atcham, opened in 1771, with the parallel 1929 bridge seen beyond. Below: the uniquely dedicated church of St Eata in Atcham.
Right top and bottom: Upton Magna is an extremely attractive village with a number of timber-framed houses and cottages grouped around the Norman church of St Lucy – another unusual dedication.

MELVERLEY

RIGHT on the Welsh border is the little timber-framed church of St Peter, pictured here basking in the sunshine of a perfect June afternoon.

To the left of the entrance porch the ground slopes steeply down to the Vyrnwy river, just upstream from its confluence with the Severn.

Inside, climb a lovely old timber staircase to a sloping gallery which gives an enjoyable view (right) of the five-light east window.

Facing page: Nearby, at Melverley Green, is another delight.
Foxglove Cottage provides one of the most "chocolate-box"
images of Shropshire!

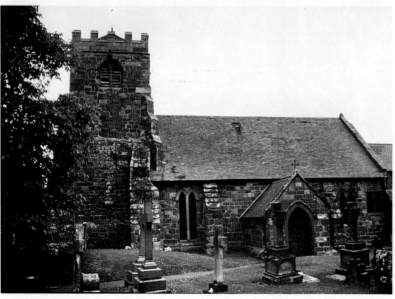

INTO BRIGAND COUNTRY!

On a sunny day in Shropshire it is easy to overlook some of the darker aspects of life in the past. A trip to Nesscliffe, visiting Little Ness and Great Ness en route is enlightening in this respect.

Little Ness has an appropriately little church (left), still mainly Norman with a bellcote. Beside it is a prominent mound surmounted by a yew tree.

Great Ness stands on a rocky outcrop. An ancient road runs down the west side of the churchyard paved only with the sloping strata of the sandstone on which the church stands.

On a heavily wooded hill here is a cave, a lair of brigands and highwaymen who ambushed travellers on the Shrewsbury to Oswestry road. As you toil upwards you might imagine them riding down the lane to intercept a coach, heavily armed and with Humphrey Kynaston at their head on his legendary horse, said to be able to leap over a man.

A convicted murderer and outlaw, Kynaston was pardoned in 1516 and lived until 1534.

The cave was inhabited until the eighteenth century, when a family of nine lived there. It is now a habitat for three species of bat.

Above: The hollow lane leading down from the brigands' cave.

Left: The left- and right-facing pistol alcoves in the cave.

Right: The worn sandstone steps to the cave entrance.

❧

LLANYBLODWEL

THIS is a delightful village, hidden in the steep-sided valley of the Afon Tanat.

Built by the vicar – the Rev John Parker – in 1850, the church and the school are both memorably idiosyncratic in design.

The tumbling river is crossed by an early-eighteenth-century bridge. A notice records that it was taken over by Shropshire County Council at the start of the twentieth century and that "ponderous vehicles" are prohibited!

At the end of the bridge stands the picturesque Horseshoe Inn and some attractive cottages.

WHITTINGTON

THE gatehouse towers (left) are the most impressive remains of this formerly extensive castle, but the whole site is accessible and enjoyable, the large ponds providing a home for a colony of noisy and apparently constantly hungry ducks.

In the background of the picture below left is the red-brick church of St John Baptist.

Below is pictured St Mary's church at Selattyn, in the extreme north-west of the county. The main part of the building is medieval, with an eighteenth-century tower and nineteenth-century transepts and north aisle.

OSWESTRY

ENTER the church precincts by the timbered lych gate in the Welsh walls and you are immediately confronted by the magnificent tower (right): it must be one of the strongest in the county. The lower part is thirteenth century, the upper storeys were rebuilt after damage suffered in the Civil War.

The lych gate was originally the entrance to the Grammar School, which has now been given a new lease of life as an enjoyable heritage centre and tearooms.

Exit into busy Church Street through the wrought-iron gates which were installed in 1738 and cross to the market square to enjoy the sculpture of a borderlands shepherd with his ram, and the colourful display outside Pickles' shop on the corner.

The town centre's most impressive timber-framed building is Llwyd Mansion, dated 1604, at the corner of Cross Street and Bailey.

EGLANTYNE JEBB

"EVERY GENERATION OF CHILDREN OFFERS MANKIND ANEW THE POSSIBILITY OF REBUILDING HIS RUIN OF A WORLD"

EGLANTYNE Jebb (1876–1928), co-founder of Save the Children with her sister Dorothy Buxton, was a remarkable woman by standards of any age.

She not only created the first international aid agency in the modern sense, but also articulated many of the concepts which were to become essential principles of modern aid work.

Born at the Lyth, near Ellesmere, she studied history at Oxford and, after finding teaching unfulfilling, travelled to Macedonia for the Macedonian Relief Fund. Here she experienced the horrors of the aftermath of war at first hand.

The First World War provided endless further widespread tragedies and on May 19, 1919, the Jebb sisters organised a large public meeting in London. The Save the Children fund was born.

The subsequent development of Save the Children throughout the seemingly endless turmoils of the twentieth century is a story of infinite inspiration. Save the Children is an organisation held in worldwide esteem; the numbers it has helped must run into

millions and, sadly, as a new century progresses will probably number many more millions before mankind matures sufficiently to live in harmony.

In her life's work, Eglantyne Jebb became not just a part of the spirit of Shropshire, but part of the spirit of humanity itself.

OSWESTRY SCENES

Right: Pickles & Co, where Church Street opens out into the square, is a riot of interesting displays, both inside and out.

Below: Oswestry Heritage Centre occupies the old Grammar School premises. The courtyard is a delightful outdoor eating area; inside (below right) are a series of exhibition rooms, including a recreation of a corner of a schoolroom in earlier days.

Lower Frankton is a small settlement around a junction on the Shropshire Union Canal. A series of locks (below) raises the southern branch of the canal to the junction level.

Contrasting bridges on the southern branch leading to Queen's Head and Maesbury. The lifting bridge gives a rather Dutch look to the surrounding marshy area; the stone bridge (below) frames the larger, flat railway bridge beyond.

CHIRK AQUEDUCT AND VIADUCT

THE boat is just leaving Shropshire and navigating into Wales. Here we are, right on the county boundary at Chirk Bank. These are splendid monuments to the canal and railway eras, major feats of civil engineering, bridging the deep gorge which marks the county boundary.

Thomas Telford built the canal aqueduct between 1796 and 1801; he had already pioneered the cast-iron trough technique at Longdon on Tern with a much more modest aqueduct. The higher railway viaduct was opened nearly 50 years later, in 1848.

Here are three more monuments to the industrial past.

Left: A lime kiln hidden in woodland at Llanymynec industrial heritage site.

Below: Oswestry locomotive sheds which now house various businesses.

Right: A disused mill, with the chimney providing a prominent landmark on the outskirts of Wem.

NORTHERN LIGHTS

The swathe of Shropshire that forms the quadrant north of the county town takes in towns such as Wem and Whitchurch, and has a completely different feel to its counterpart in the south. Flatter and more industrial in its origins, it is no less fascinating.

AT Wem, the tower of St Peter and St Paul dominates the High Street. It is the earliest remaining part of the church, approached by wrought-iron gates. Further ironwork is found inside on the pulpit. The nave and chancel were rebuilt in the nineteenth century.

ADAMS' College at Wem was founded by Sir Thomas Adams in 1650 and rebuilt in 1776 – the style we see today.

The impressive entrance gates are a memorial to old boys of the school who died in the First World War.

THE tower of St Michael's church at Loppington is Perpendicular period, the same age as the south aisle to the right.

The timbered porch of 1658 gives a good introduction to the splendid beamed roofs inside in both the south aisle and the nave.

SCENES THAT CAUGHT THE EYE

A RICHLY timbered house at Prees (left) is of apparently complex construction, probably encompassing two periods of enlargement and culminating in a fine jettied facade to the street.

An Elizabethan barn at West Felton (below left) has an impressive internal structure.

Early morning in Wem High Street (below) shows what a difference is made to an urban scene by trees and flower baskets.

TILSTOCK

CLIVE

ELLESMERE

CHRIST Church at Tilstock was completed in 1835, built of red brick with the window frames made unusually from cast iron. The early morning sky graphically outlines the steeply pitched roof of the slender tower.

AT Clive, the soaring spire of All Saints is visible from afar. It is a grand church, both architecturally and in its furnishings; a fitting centrepiece for a delightful village in a lovely setting.

ST Mary's church tower is the dominant feature on the town skyline viewed from the meadows beside the Mere. The tower is at the crossing of the large church and is the oldest part; the majority of the building was restored in successive phases in the nineteenth century.

RESTFUL SCENES

Right: The view across the Mere from the waterside gardens at Ellesmere.

Below: A picturesque cottage close by Ellesmere church.

Below right: An evening view across White Mere from Spunhill.

Facing page (clockwise from left):
St Swithin's church at Cheswardine is particularly rewarding for its collection of 1890s stained glass and the fine early English chapel.

A view along Cheswardine's village street from the entrance to the church.

Holy Trinity at Calverhall is an impressive church, again with enjoyable nineteenth-century windows. The setting of the church is greatly enhanced by the immaculate bowling green next to the churchyard.

A BUSTLING TOWN

WHITCHURCH is a bustling and attractive town, with numerous appealing streets and alleys lined with impressive timber-framed and Georgian buildings.

Shown on this page are two buildings which particularly catch the attention: the imposing facade of the NatWest building – imitation, yet an appropriate addition to the town centre; and the real thing, a traditional building containing a traditional baker's shop with a window full of tempting delights.

It is, however, St Alkmund's Church which provides the highlight of a visit to the town. The exterior has a majestic tower, but the interior is literally breathtaking. This is Shropshire's largest eighteenth-century church outside Shrewsbury and only an elevated view from the large tiered gallery can encompass the scale of the nave, with its soaring Tuscan columns and arches leading to the ornate apse.

Whitchurch is also a town of clocks. It is the home of J B Joyce and Company, the oldest firm of tower clockmakers in the world, trading since William Joyce began making clocks in 1690. The company moved to Whitchurch in 1834, occupying new premises in Station Road in 1904 with its own electricity generator, from where it has traded ever since.

The four-sided clock of 1994 which stands in the centre of Whitchurch.

CLOCKMAKERS THROUGH FOURTEEN REIGNS

BY the mid-Victorian period, J B Joyce had more than 150 years of clockmaking experience and an unrivalled reputation for quality of workmanship. The huge expansion of all forms of commerce and transport, the building boom in town halls, universities and company headquarters, and the widespread church renovation movement, all combined to create unprecedented demand for public clocks.

Locally, many new clocks were installed. In 1855 a clock for the Market House at Shrewsbury occasioned many complimentary comments; it was illuminated by four gas jets adjustable to the length of the hours of darkness. When the new Market Hall was built, Joyces supplied the clock for that too, in 1870.

Prestige commissions were obtained throughout the country. Nine cathedrals were fitted with Joyce clocks, including Salisbury in 1884, while the new clock replaced one that had been installed five centuries earlier in 1384! But it was not just in Great Britain that Joyce clocks were installed: by the end of the nineteenth century, Lord Grimthorpe – the country's leading authority on clocks – declared Messrs Joyce to be "the foremost manufacturers of clocks in the Empire".

When Norman Joyce retired in 1965 after more than 50 years of service, it marked the end of eight generations of the family which had produced 25 clock- and watchmakers trading in Whitchurch, Denbigh and Ruthin and, in earlier days, Dublin and New York. J B Joyce then merged with John Smith and Sons of Derby but clockmaking has continued in Whitchurch and the town continues to take pride in calling itself "The home of tower clocks".

Grinshill is a beautifully kept village. Many of the buildings and walls are constructed of massive sandstone blocks. Above is a traditional cottage on the corner of Gooseberry Lane. Below is All Saints Church (1840) with its slender Italianate tower.

Above is a view of a house and garden typical of this exceptionally attractive village. The village is backed by Corbet Wood (below), named after the family of nearby Acton Reynald.

St Bartholomew: Moreton Corbet

THE tower was begun in the 1530s and not completed until 1769.

The enjoyment of a visit to this charming church is greatly added to if the bells are being rung.

Examples of most periods of architecture are in evidence, from Norman through to the nineteenth century, but a visit is chiefly memorable for the extraordinary collection of monuments to the Corbet family. The earliest is dated 1513; the most recent to Vincent Corbet who died at 13 and whose monument was erected in 1904.

The whole setting is delightful, with the ruins of the castle in an adjacent field.

MORETON CORBET CASTLE

SPECTACULAR is the only adequate description of these ruins (opposite) for the impression that they make on the first-time visitor. On a sunny June evening, and viewed across the field from the drive leading to the church, the ruins looked like a dramatic stage set. A small group of figures playing cricket against one wall serves to show the scale of what had once been one of Shropshire's great houses.

The oldest part is the late Norman keep, constructed around 1200 and shown in the picture opposite behind the tree. To the right and in front of the keep are the castle buildings and curtain wall. This was, however, a grand house in Elizabethan times as well as a castle. Clearly with the threat from Welsh border raids having passed into history, the Corbets felt able to build a more commodious residence, which was commenced in 1579.

Unfortunately, the peaceful years did not last; this time the threat came from within England, in the Civil War. A Parliamentarian siege resulted in the destruction of both castle and house in 1644.

Today we have one of the country's most dramatic ruins and a major evocation of the spirit of Shropshire in the four centuries preceding the Civil War.

A MILLENNIUM MONOLITH!

AT Stoke on Tern, in the Glebe Field next to the churchyard, there is delightful tree-planting and an inscribed monolith which commemorated the millennium. It is unusual and imaginative encounters such as this which make a place memorable.

The church of St Peter (left) was completed in 1875 and has a fairly unusual layout with a south aisle, on the left, almost as large as the nave, and the tower placed at the south-west corner of the aisle.

This was another area where the Corbet influence was strong. An impressive monument to Sir Reginald Corbet of 1566 is one of the most striking interior features.

A STUDY IN BLACK AND WHITE

PETSEY is a historic house on the bank of the River Tern. The house belongs to 1634 and makes an attractive picture beside the little river – especially when complemented by this contented herd of Friesians.

WOLLERTON OLD HALL GARDENS

THIS garden was started by the owners John and Lesley Jenkins in 1984. As these pictures show, there is a series of separate gardens, based on appealing to the senses and emotions through viewpoints, vistas and contrasts.

Each "room" has individual planting and atmosphere: roses, a yew walk, a rock garden and a Gertrude Jekyll-inspired herbaceous border.

Beyond the area of walled gardens is a less formal area on the slope to the River Tern.

The whole complex can be the basis of a delightful afternoon in the search for the spirit of Shropshire.

HODNET HALL GARDENS

HODNET Hall is the home of Mr and Mrs Algernon Heber-Percy, and its gardens are nationally renowned. There have been park and gardens at Hodnet for many centuries, developed from the three different sites on which the family has built successive houses.

The current gardens are based on a series of beautiful pools initiated by Brigadier Heber-Percy in the 1920s. The planting schemes subsequently developed have aimed to provide a show of colour throughout the seasons. Early spring arrives with blossom and vast swathes of daffodils, followed by rhododendrons, azaleas, laburnum, lilac and bluebells in the wooded area around the top pools.

In summer the borders are at their peak, accompanied by masses of hydrangeas and followed by late-summer shrubs. Autumn is a quiet, magical time when the gardens are ablaze with turning leaves and berries.

Hodnet's gardens are unforgettable, an evocation not just of the spirit of Shropshire but of the whole tradition of British gardening. From April to September, no one can wander through the ever-changing vistas and fail to be enchanted and uplifted by the experience.

Top left: Unusual chimneys at Hodnet.

Left: Timbered buildings in the village.

Facing page: The main pool at Hodnet Hall and the house's south facade shown to best advantage on a sunny day.

HAWKSTONE PARK

"UNIQUE" can be an overworked word, but a walk through the fantasy landscape of Hawkstone Park really is like no other walk: the visitor becomes completely immersed in an other-worldly landscape, lost in a time-warp. No wonder the BBC's search for The Land of Narnia ended here!

The landscaping and creation of the walks and follies were begun in the latter half of the eighteenth century by Sir Rowland Hill, and continued after his death in 1783 by his son Sir Richard. They espoused the wilder aspects of the picturesque landscape – often termed "sublime". Wild precipitous crags, deep ravines and tumbling streams were all essential elements of a sublime landscape, and Hawkstone provided an ideal setting with its craggy cliffs of red sandstone. It was a similar concept to that created by Thomas Johnes from neighbouring north Herefordshire when he established his ill-fated paradise at Hafod in Mid Wales.

Hawkstone became famous throughout the country as soon as it was completed and attracted a constant procession of visitors including Dr Johnson and the Duke of Wellington; the latter is commemorated in a scene in the White Tower, discussing the battle plans before Waterloo.

English Heritage has designated Hawkstone a Grade-I historic landscape and Shropshire is fortunate to have this semi-mystical place hidden deep in its countryside.

Follies, monuments and immense natural grandeur . . . these pictures show Hawkstone Park in all its magnificence.

MARKET DRAYTON

WHAT cold be more appropriate than to arrive, purely by chance, in Market Drayton on market day? The multicoloured stall awnings and lively throng of eager shoppers are a sight to behold. It gives the same atmosphere that one encounters in a provincial French market town: the shouts of the vegetable and fruit vendors, the smell of roasting and cooking, and the hubbub of eager bargain-hunters.

The market stretched from the square into neighbouring streets and round into another square outside the Butter Market.

Above: The Wharf.
Below: Tyrley Cut, on the Shropshire Union Canal near Market Drayton is the longest and deepest canal cutting in Europe.

The Church of St Mary soars above the neighbouring buildings and dominates the views of the town from most directions.

CLIVE OF INDIA

FROM TEENAGE TEARAWAY TO PEER OF THE REALM

IF only a portion of the misdemeanours ascribed to young Robert Clive (b. 1725) were true, he would today be a prime candidate for a social behavioural order.

While a pupil at Market Drayton, he gained a reputation for dreadful behaviour throughout the community: he was expelled, followed by further expulsions from schools in London and Hertfordshire.

No doubt driven to the point of despair, Robert's father obtained a position for his son in the East India Company in Madras. Thus it was at 17 years of age, Robert Clive set sail for India and a life of boredom and misery that led to a failed suicide attempt after some months in India.

Salvation was at hand, however. Hostilities between the French and the East India Company provided Robert Clive with the opportunity to distinguish himself and gain promotion. Simultaneously, he commenced trading on his own account and prospered financially to the extent that he was able to return to Shropshire in 1753 as a fairly affluent black-sheep-made-good. He married and renovated the family house.

A further tour of duty in India brought increasing military and financial success to Clive, but his dealings with Indian princes, and ruthless methods in business, made him numerous powerful enemies. By the time he returned finally to Shropshire in 1760 he was a seriously rich man and purchased two estates: Walcot at Lydbury North and Oakley Park near Ludlow.

He was awarded an Irish peerage, taking the title Baron Plassey (this referred to the place in India where he defeated the ruler of Bengal after the notorious "black hole of Calcutta" incident. In 1761 he was elected MP for Shrewsbury and subsequently became the town's mayor.

Clive's later years were plagued by increasing ill health and drug dependency, and by a prolonged campaign waged against him by enemies from his days in India. parliament debated the charges levelled against him on several occasions, and finally decided that he had been guilty of accepting bribes from Indian rulers. No action was taken, however, because of his key role in establishing British rule in India.

Robert Clive died at his London home at the age of 49, having secured a place in the history of British imperial expansion to the extent that he has always been referred to as Clive of India.

The Tudor House Hotel is a prime example of a timber-framed hostelry, which can be found appropriately busy on market day.

A quieter scene down the hill where the canal wharf has now found a new lease of life catering for the thriving waterborne leisure industry.

A Quiet Summer Evening at Weston-under-Redcastle

EASTERN PROMISE

It has been a hot summer day, and Shropshire is bathed in evening sunshine. Looking towards the West Midlands from the east of the county, tall cumulus clouds are forming as the heat rises from that vast conurbation.

AROUND NEWPORT

AN ELEGANT TOWN

THE long, wide High Street runs south-east from the former canal basin and has a fascinating variety of buildings of all periods, from medieval to nineteenth century. The centrepiece is the main town church, which stands midway on an island formed by the curving St Mary's Street.

The two pictures on the left-hand of the facing page shows Georgian and early Victorian shops in St Mary's Street. Upper right is the former market square with the butter cross. The impressive south facade and tower of St Nicholas's Church are of red sandstone, substantially restored in the latter half of the nineteenth century. The lower right picture shows the brick-built National School of 1840 and the schoolhouse. The school is still in use, serving the community of Church Aston, now a southern suburb of Newport.

This page shows two contrasting buildings on opposite sides of the High Street. Above left is a very well preserved timber-framed townhouse of 1667 with a Gothic tower added on the corner in the early nineteenth century. Above right is the Italianate facade of the Town Hall of 1860, topped with a clock surrounded by garlands and, again, very well preserved.

Newport is on the extreme eastern boundary of Shropshire. Always busy and bustling it lies to the east of the distinctive area of the Weald Moors, views of which are shown on the next two pages.

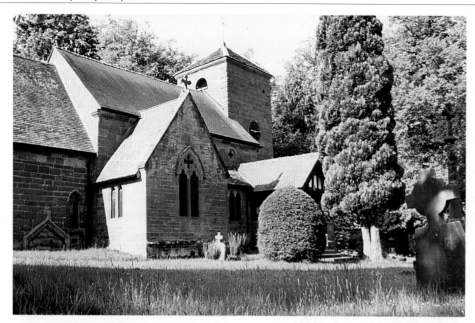

Facing page (clockwise from top left): St Milburga's Church in Beckbury is an attractive church in delightful surroundings. The nave and tower are Georgian; the chancel, on the left, is of around 1300, restored in 1884.
St Peter's Church, Edgmond has a Perpendicular tower which dominates the village.
Kynnersley is a pretty village in the heart of Weald Moors country.
Idsall House at Shifnal, pleasantly framed by lilac and laburnum, is thought to be the oldest house in the town.

This page (clockwise from top left): Telford's aqueduct of 1794 carried the Shropshire Union Canal over the Tern at Longdon – the first cast-iron aqueduct constructed.
Crudgington Moor: this view shows the peaty nature of the soil.
Lilleshall's church of St Michael has a late Norman nave and a tower in the Perpendicular style. It stands in a large churchyard overlooked by a nineteenth-century monument on a rocky hill.
Wrockwardine is a hill village above the Tern and moors. The houses crowd closely around St Peter's church.

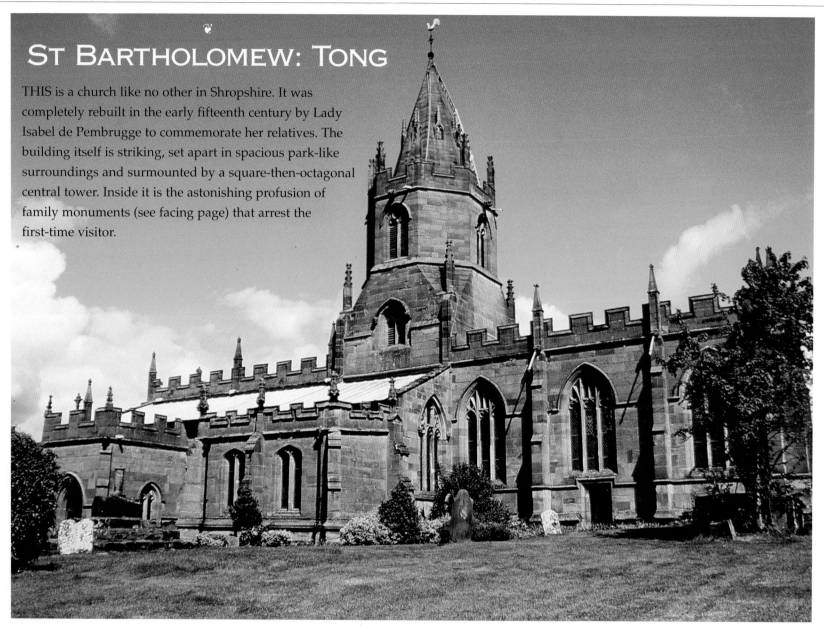

St Bartholomew: Tong

THIS is a church like no other in Shropshire. It was completely rebuilt in the early fifteenth century by Lady Isabel de Pembrugge to commemorate her relatives. The building itself is striking, set apart in spacious park-like surroundings and surmounted by a square-then-octagonal central tower. Inside it is the astonishing profusion of family monuments (see facing page) that arrest the first-time visitor.

THE monuments commemorate the Vernon and Stanley families, holders of high offices of state and patrons of Shakespeare. They provide an unrivalled stylistic sequence of the late middle ages, from early fifteenth century to late elizabethan. Shown (left to right) are just three of this outstanding collection: Sir Richard Vernon; Sir Richard Stanley; and Sir Harry Vernon.

A Spring Morning in East Shropshire

ALBRIGHTON and Donnington started as little neighbouring hamlets on opposite sides of a brook. Donnington has remained as a few houses grouped around its church; Albrighton has expanded greatly into a small town with a long High Street.

The pictures show (upper left) the recently created streamside walk at St Cuthbert's Meadow by Donnington church, and (lower left) the green at the eastern end of Albrighton High Street.

Facing page (clockwise from top left): St Mary's Church, Sheriffhales; two examples of attractive timber-framed houses which sit in the residential area around the church; and a delightful cottage facing the church at Tong.

LITTLE WENLOCK

THE village stands near the Wrekin. The picture, left, shows the southern slope in evening sunshine.

The Church of St Lawrence is really two churches side by side. Pictured below it has a Victorian brick-built nave of 1865 and a tower of 1667. Just visible between them can be seen the earlier nave roof.

The picture below left, taken in the evening sunshine of a mid-May evening and showing a clematis in full bloom, typifies the charm of Little Wenlock.

A Gem From the Past

FOLLOW a long, winding road up a hidden valley to reach Upton Cressett. Two wonderful rewards lay in wait: St Michael's church (see page 35) and Upton Hall (pictured).

The hall is a brick-built Tudor mansion which towers over the little churchyard. To the left is the unusual detached gatehouse with its two polygonal turrets.

SUNSET ON THE SEVERN

IN these two views, taken from the same spot just east of Leighton, a late burst of sunlight on a May evening is captured. Dark storm clouds were moving away and the sunlight was moving along the Severn valley.

On this page is Buildwas power station, more than two miles downstream from the camera position, but showing the play of sunlight on its vast cooling towers. The structure is caught in a small spotlight; Benthall Edge wood, behind the structures, is still in shade.

Opposite is the view downhill from the camera position; a classic textbook meander of the Severn below the estate of Leighton Hall. The storm clouds can be seen receding, again providing just a brief window of sunshine to highlight the riverbanks, with much of the woodland of Buildwas Park still in deep shadow.

Ironbridge: the town is terraced up the steep side of the gorge to St Luke's Church (1836).

WHERE THE MODERN WORLD TOOK SHAPE

THE IRONBRIDGE GORGE AND COALBROOKDALE

"The most extraordinary district in the world" was how one writer described the Severn Gorge in 1837, the year of Victoria's ascension. Almost 150 years later UNESCO agreed by conferring the coveted designation of World Heritage Site on Ironbridge Gorge, thereby including it on a list that contained the Taj Mahal and the Grand Canyon.

What this designation recognised was that, here in Ironbridge Gorge, inventions and processes began the whole new phase of modern developments which came to be collectively termed the "industrial revolution". Modern industrial society had its catalyst on the eastern edge of a county still known for its generally rural ambience.

When Nikolaus Pevsner visited the area in 1957 to compile the Shropshire volume of his *Buildings of England* series, he described the area around the warehouse and early furnace as "shockingly sordid" and observed, with extraordinary prescience, that "A little money could put it right and create a monument to early English industry."

If only he could see it now! Coalbrookdale and Ironbridge have benefited not from "a little money" but from a capital investment of millions of pounds, to create a monument to early industrial development unparalleled anywhere else in the world.

THE GORGE MUSEUMS

HERE on the southern edge of the former East Shropshire Coalfield is a unique concentration of 10 museums interpreting the long history of industrial development in this beautiful setting.

Coalbrookdale contains Enginuity and the Museum of Iron, as well as two Darby houses – Rosehill and Dale House – and the nearby Quaker burial ground. This was the heart of the Darby empire. Down where the dale meets the main gorge is the extraordinary Gothic warehouse which houses the Museum of the Gorge.

Downstream along the Severn are the Tollhouse, accommodating a display on the history of the Iron Bridge; the Coalport China Museum; and the nearby Tar Tunnel. Up another wooded tributary valley is Blists Hill Victorian Town with factories, shops, pubs and houses, where costumed staff and volunteers recreate the authentic atmosphere of nineteenth-century life.

Across the river is the Broseley Pipeworks, which closed in 1957, and Jackfield Tile Works, where the tradition of encaustic tile-making is kept alive by skilled craftspeople in the original buildings.

Nowhere else in the world is there such a comprehensive collection of museums which, together with their associated small towns, make a visit to Ironbridge Gorge a highlight of the quest to find the spirit of Shropshire.

The Iron Bridge: created in 1779 by Abraham Darby III, it was the first cast-iron bridge in the world.

THOSE MEN OF IRON

THE FOUNDING FATHERS

WHEN the early Darbys held sway at Coalbrookdale, people came from throughout Europe to learn about the groundbreaking technology which they were developing, and the Iron Bridge became a tourist attraction in its own right. Coalbrookdale was the Silicon Valley of the late eighteenth century; the most famous and successful industrial area in Great Britain.

"The cradle of the industrial revolution" is a frequently used phrase for explaining and marketing the area, and this inevitably conjures up images of the Victorians and the Great Exhibition of 1851. These impressions are likely to be reinforced by visiting Blists Hill Victorian Town and the Museum of Iron, which features much of the ornamental ironwork produced by the company for the Victorian consumer market.

It is when we look at the dates of the early Darby men who founded and developed the iron-making industry that we realise what a long process of technological development it was. Abraham Darby I was born in 1678 . . . just 27 years after the Civil War. The son of a Quaker locksmith in Dudley, he moved to Bristol in 1699 and entered the brass-making trade.

Darby moved north to Shropshire in 1708, following other Bristol Quaker brassworkers, but he was seeking to manufacture cooking pots in a cheaper material: cast iron. After a year in Coalbrookdale he succeeded in attempts to smelt iron with charcoal, using the local

Blists Hill Victorian Town: looking towards the blast furnaces.

HE DARBY DYNASTY

low-sulphur coal from the East Shropshire Coalfield. He sold his pots at markets and fairs, and the business expanded steadily. Darby was in poor health, however, and died prematurely at 39 in 1717.

Abraham II, his son, was only six years old, and the business was put into the hands of Richard Ford, a family member, and Thomas Golding, a Quaker merchant from Bristol. They proved extremely capable managers and the foundry expanded steadily through several major developments, including the manufacture of iron cylinders for steam engines.

Abraham Darby II did not become a full partner until 1742, but for the next 21 years he continued the vigorous expansion of the company's activities, opening new foundries outside Coalbrookdale valley, at Horsehay and Ketley. This initiated a phase of expansion for the whole East Shropshire Coalfield area.

Once again, history was repeated. Abraham II died in 1763 at 52 years of age when his son was just 13, and again a son-in-law assumed control. This was another extremely businesslike Bristol Quaker who managed the company well for five years until Abraham III took control in 1768 at the age of 18.

Abraham III was to have only 21 years, like his father, and he was to die at 39 like his grandfather. But in those 21 years he took Coalbrookdale forward to become the most famous industrial area in Great Britain, and manufactured the Iron Bridge, destined to become an icon of the industrial revolution.

The Museum of Iron. John Bell's Boy and Swan fountain from the 1851 Great Exhibition, and the Great Warehouse clock tower.

❦
CHANGING FORTUNES

THE fortunes of the Darby family and of the whole East Shropshire Coalfield reached their height in the 30 years following the construction of the Iron Bridge. Other iron bridges were made for locations throughout the British Isles and beyond; a high-pressure steam engine was made for Richard Trevithick's first steam railway locomotive; across the river in Broseley John Wilkinson made the first iron boat (1787) and Telford's iron aqueduct over the River Tern was built in 1796. These were also the years of the Napoleonic War and, despite their Quaker convictions, the Darbys profited along with all other iron producers.

Then after Waterloo in 1815, came peace and a drastic fall in the demand for iron. To add to the difficulties facing Coalbrookdale, other regions such as the Black Country and South Wales were increasingly providing fierce competition. By 1818 the Coalbrookdale furnaces were shut down and the area was in depression.

Now a fourth-generation Darby stepped forwards to revive the company's fortunes. Francis Darby, younger son of Abraham III took over the Coalbrookdale works and began to specialise in fine-art castings for the home and garden, and larger items such as park gates, railings and fountains. In the 1851 Great Exhibition the Coalbrookdale Company had huge success – although Francis failed to see it, dying in 1850 after 30 years spent pulling the company back from financial extinction in the early 1820s.

Coalport China Museum. John Rose opened these works around 1792 and the firm lasted until 1926.

THE Great Exhibition, then, represented the high Victorian heyday of Coalbrookdale. It was the world's largest foundry employing around 3,000 and with a weekly output of 2,000 tons.

It is mainly the products of this second period of worldwide fame that we see in the Museum of Iron today. The Darby dynasty continued its association with the Coalbrookdale Company until 1925, a period of 217 years since Abraham Darby I arrived in the valley seeking his fortune in the reign of Queen Anne.

It was the flair, vision and dynamism of the Darbys that shaped the lives of thousands in this part of the county, for more than two centuries. The Darbys made Coalbrookdale known worldwide, and their achievements have now been encompassed in a World Heritage Site. They certainly played a major role in creating the spirit of Shropshire.

Above: The Museum of the Gorge occupies this Gothic building built by the Coalbrookdale Company.
Right: Pipemaker Rex Key at the Broseley Pipeworks.

ALL SAINTS: BROSELEY

THE size of the church reflects the importance of Broseley in the early nineteenth century. It was the main town of the East Shropshire Coalfield and the home of John Wilkinson, noted ironmaster of the late eighteenth century. He installed the first steam engine built by Boulton and Watt for use outside their own premises at Birmingham.

MADELEY CENTRE

MADELEY, a former small town of the coalfield, is now incorporated into Telford. The shopping centre is built around the Anstice Memorial Institute of 1868. The tomb of R R Anstice is in St Michael's church, built by Thomas Telford in 1796.

❦

JACKFIELD BRIDGE

THIS dramatically futuristic bridge was opened in the early 1990s on the site of the first toll-free crossing of the Severn in the area, which was opened in 1909.

Jackfield is a fascinating area for industrial history enthusiasts, with a number of early industrial premises and houses still to be seen.

Together with neighbouring Coalport, Jackfield formed the downstream extension of riverside industrial settlements.

TELFORD: MODERN MELTING POT

❦ Neither the Romans nor the Normans changed Shropshire as much as Telford Development Corporation did when it built the county's new town!

After a brief spell as Dawley, from 1963, the government of the day decided to go for broke and virtually doubled the area in 1968, with the mining/ironfounding towns of Ironbridge, Madeley and Dawley (birthplace of Captain Webb – see his monument) being joined by Oakengates and Hadley, so that the town took in pretty well all the East Shropshire Coalfield.

The odd one out was Wellington, a traditional country town and agricultural centre with a market established by royal charter in 1244. Wellington has a strong affinity with its neighbouring hill, The Wrekin, which gives its name to a famous local toast associated with the Pointon family.

The name Telford was the personal choice of the then Minister of Housing and Local Government, Anthony Greenwood, who, noting that Brunel had his name attached to a university, wanted to immortalise the name of Great Britain's other great civil engineer.

The modern glass exterior of Darby House typifies the "feel" of Telford as a modern, thriving community.

The idea of having a new town in east Shropshire has been claimed by many but the most deserving claim is probably that of a local journalist, "Scoop" Bowdler, the Dawley correspondent of the *Birmingham Gazette*, in which he wrote a piece in February 1955 urging: ". . . here's the place for overspill". His rationale, accepted by government later on, was that the dereliction of 300 years of old industry could be cleared up at the same time – a task well beyond the resources of any local authority.

The town is now a buoyant society, in which the old population of around 65,000 has, for 40 years or so, mingled with and often married the immigrants from all around the UK – and indeed from much of the rest of the world.

THOMAS TELFORD

INSPIRATION FOR A NEW TOWN

A NATIVE of Dumfriesshire, Thomas Telford initially served as an apprentice stonemason, but wished to widen his horizons and seek more rewarding employment opportunities.

He moved to Edinburgh in 1780 to study buildings and other civil works, and then to London two years later. He was now 25 and had both practical and theoretical skills to offer; he hoped to find commissions as an architect.

Telford was successful remarkably quickly, working on Somerset House, then Portsmouth Dockyard. A meeting with Sir William Pulteney, MP for Shrewsbury who was a native of Telford's own parish in Scotland, brought Telford to Shrewsbury where he initially became involved in two major projects: the renovation of the castle and the construction of a new prison. In 1787 he was appointed county surveyor of public works for Shropshire. He had come a long way both literally and figuratively since leaving Scotland five years earlier.

Telford had made the transition from architect to civil engineer, but always with a

sound practical background of building – particularly with stone. Evidence of his far-reaching skills can be seen throughout Shropshire, but his county surveyorship was only a small part of his responsibilities and achievements. Canals, roads, bridges and dockyards throughout Great Britain, and the Gotha Canal in Sweden all bear testament to his consummate skill and apparently

limitless energy at the peak of his life.

When you drive across the Menai Bridge of boat along Pontcysyllte Aqueduct you are making use of memorials to the pioneering engineer. The A5 road is almost as he surveyed and laid it, as is the Caledonian Canal and the greater part of the highland road network in Scotland. Telford's pre-eminence in his profession was recognised in his lifetime: he was made first president of the Institution of Civil Engineers in 1820. When he died in 1834 he was buried among the nation's revered figures in Westminster Abbey.

Shropshire certainly cannot forget its debt to Thomas Telford, providing his greatest memorial of all in naming its new town after him 130 years after his death.

A NEW generation of young people with roots on both sides now proudly regards itself as simply *Telfordian*. Famous representatives of Telford might be Billy Wright (old community – Ironbridge) and Ritchie Woodhall (new community – Woodside). Other examples are Sir Gordon Richards, Dr William Withering (who discovered that digitalis could ease heart disease) and Patrick Brontë, brother of Emily, Charlotte and Anne, who did a spell as curate of All Saints in wellington. Unlike his sisters he was, it seems, something of a *roué*!

The people give Telford its distinctive

FORGING AN IDENTITY

spirit and sense of community. The opening of the town's own commercial radio station, Telford FM, in 1999 and the award of borough status to the unitary Telford & Wrekin Council in 2002 gave the whole town an even greater sense of closeness.

But this is the most astonishing of new towns. Madeley Court – now a hotel – is a magnificent Elizabethan house with a Jacobean gatehouse, and it sits in an estate

whose ownership can be traced back to before the Norman conquest. Its most famous resident was Abraham Darby III who, just down the road, built the world's first iron bridge, over the Severn in 1779. The bridge, giving its name to its surrounding township, became a tourist attraction from the day it opened to traffic and is the centrepiece of the whole Ironbridge Gorge World Heritage Site.

The industry has long gone from the Gorge but the eternal severn still runs peacefully through – in summer at least – the banks on each side lined by earnest fishermen watched by throngs of visitors.

TOWN OF SURPRISES

THE British army's main ordnance depot was established at the other end of town, in Donnington, before the Second World War. Its museum has some Luftwaffe reconnaisance photographs of it, all precisely annotated in red ink, although it was never actually bombed. A curious distinction is that it houses the Russian cannon, captured in the Crimean War, from which Victoria crosses are cast.

The new face of Telford also has its surprises. This is *the* town in the UK in which to find Japanese companies. Toyota in Derbyshire might be the UK's biggest but Telford has Maxell, Ricoh, Denso and some 15 or 20 others employing thousands. Tatung, Mitac and Enta Technologies of Taiwan add to the far-eastern flavour. These and hundreds of new companies from the UK and the rest of the world – 15 overseas countries are represented here – have helped to create a second industrial revolution, 300 years after the first.

The centrepiece of the town is a park of 450 acres which is preserved from development, right in the centre. You can walk out of the shopping malls straight into it. There are lakes – one with a Greek amphitheatre built into its bankside – ornamental gardens, a show arena, woodlands and Wonderland: a place to take small children to see what their nursery rhymes might translate to in "reality". You can even have a birthday at the Mad Hatter's tea party! And one of those lakes harbours some long-ago imported European catfish, which have been recorded at up to 16 feet in the Danube delta, and are highly predatory (though not indulging much beyond frogs and ducklings here).

For something more energetic, Telford Ice Rink was opened by the Princess Royal in 1984. Telford International Centre is the place for indoor racquets courts (it hosted the British Tennis Championships for many years) but has another life as one of Britain's top ten conference and exhibition centres, bringing millions of pounds into the local economy.

And there is a long tradition of crown green bowls (usually on greens attached to pubs), local cricket and local football. Telford United (formerly the "lilywhites" of Wellington Town are one of the better-known non-league sides.

DAVID EVERINGTON AND PAMELA BRADBURN

Facing page: The Japanese garden in Telford Town Park, and the Enta Technologies pagoda.

Left: Telford Superbowl.

THE HAPPY EXPLORERS

Kathleen and Barry Freeman count themselves fortunate that they have complementary interests which enable them to produce books such as this. Kathleen takes the pictures; her extensive art training gives her the eye for composition which creates so many memorable and evocative pictures. Barry plans the journeys, undertakes background research and writes the text.

Both are former teachers: Kathleen taught art, Barry taught geography and environmental studies, and is the holder of a royal award for services to environmental education. Both enjoy travelling and especially discovering out-of-the-way places off the beaten track.

As long-term residents of neighbouring north Herefordshire, Kathleen and Barry have a familiarity with and affection for Shropshire, stretching back many years. To finally make the time necessary to travel the length and breadth of the county in detail fulfilled a long-term ambition.

This is the fifth such book they have created together. It is hoped that all who know and love Shropshire, and those who are only just discovering its delights will feel that this book does the county justice, and encourages people to further explore this remarkably diverse borderlands county.

Happy exploring!

PLACES OPEN TO THE PUBLIC

MOST places featured in this book have opening hours that vary seasonally and which can also change from year to year. We have therefore given the telephone numbers so that interested readers can establish up-to-date arrangements for themselves.

All establishments publish leaflets and/or advertise in tourist publications. We have therefore also provided the telephone numbers of tourist information centres. An increasing number of establishments maintain websites.

There are, of course, may other places of interest to visit within the county, details of which can also be obtained from tourist information centres. The information provided here is correct at the time of publication of this book.

TOURIST INFORMATION CENTRES

Bridgnorth	01746 763257
Church Stretton	01694 723133
Ellesmere	01691 622981
Ironbridge	01952 432166
Ludlow	01584 875053
Market Drayton	01630 652139
Much Wenlock	01952 727679
Oswestry Town	01691 662753
Oswestry Mile End	01691 662488
Shrewsbury	01743 281200
Telford	01952 230032
Whitchurch	01948 664577

INDIVIDUAL ESTABLISHMENTS
NT = NATIONAL TRUST
EH = ENGLISH HERITAGE

Acton Scott Historic Working Farm Museum	01694 781306
Attingham Park, NT	01743 708162
Benthall Hall, NT	01952 882159
Boscobel House, EH	01902 850244
Buildwas Abbey, EH	01952 433274
Burford House Gardens	01584 810777
Daniel's Mill	01746 762753
Dudmaston Hall, NT	01746 780866
English Nature	01948 880362
Haughmond Abbey, EH	01743 709661
Hawstone Park and Follies	01939 200611
Hodnet Hall Gardens	01630 685202
Ironbridge Gorge Museums	01952 432166
Ludlow Castle	01584 873355
Severn Valley Railway	01299 403816
Shropshire Wildlife Trust	01743 241691
Stokesay Castle, EH	01588 672544
Sunnycroft, NT	01952 242884
Wenlock Priory, EH	01952 727466
Wollerton Old Hall Gardens	01630 685760
Wroxeter Roman City, EH	01743 761330

Note: Churches featured which are in the care of the Churches Conservation Trust are either always open or there is a keyholder nearby.

❧

ACKNOWLEDGEMENTS

KATHLEEN and Barry Freeman owe a great debt of gratitude to the large number of people who have helped in the compilation of this book: the staff and custodians of properties in the care of the major national organisations; owners of gardens and other properties; staff of local authorities, particularly the tourist information centres; owners of companies; and the innumerable chance acquaintances they met in a thousand miles of travelling, spread over 18 months.

The vast majority of the photographs were taken by Kathleen Freeman specifically for this book. Most of the photographs of the featured properties listed were supplied by the organisations and individual owners.

Shropshire Newspapers provided a number of additional photographs and portraits. The portrait of Eglantyne Jebb was from the archives of Save the Children.

The research and text is by Barry Freeman, except for specific features where authorship in acknowledged in those features. Barry is particularly grateful to Pam Bradburn of Telford & Wrekin Community Trust, a friend of long standing who provided invaluable help and contacts.

The feature on Ironbridge and Coalbrookdale was compiled from information and pictures kindly supplied by Richard Aldred and Barbara Taylor of the Ironbridge Gorge Museums Trust.

INDEX